To Usha
with love

CONTENTS

MAPS

PLATES

Between pages 74 and 75

Street scenes in Jandiali: local vegetable vendor (above);
   enjoying sugar cane (below)

Ganda Singh (extreme right): 90-year-old returnee

Prospective emigrants: one member of family already in England

Immigrant pedlars

Émigré: training to be a nurse

Akhand path

Indian Youth Federation meeting

Punjabi field instead of rose garden: Gravesindian backyard

House sold to Gravesindian: The Avenue

Pukka houses and bungalows built with emigrant money

Cooking: in the village (above); in Gravesindia (below)

Jandiali 1978: almost a ghost village

Tube-well in Jandiali: built with pounds sterling

PREFACE

The immigration of former colonial subjects into Great Britain has increasingly become a matter of grave concern. Although people from the entire subcontinent of India have emigrated to all parts of Great Britain, this study focuses on one of these groups and on one location: the Sikh Jats (farmers) who left their Punjabi villages to settle in the city of Gravesend in Kent. An examination of their process of adaptation discloses the vast circumstantial changes they have encountered and the socio-political tensions they have generated in the host community.

These Sikhs originate from a small-scale peasant society where resources and self-esteem stem from birth, land and kinsmen. Initially, their concerns were limited to their villages, where the society was divided into groups with specialized functions determined by birth. The dominant high caste Jats, a proud people, have always controlled the land, economic resources, and political activities in their villages. Being a landowner has always been a symbol of 'Jatness' and royalty. Hence, emigrating to England signalled a profound change. The move has thrust them into a large-scale industrial society where farming is not a viable alternative for their livelihood, and where they have to depend on the English for jobs. In their new environment, their world view has to include concerns outside their own group. Their self-image has also changed since they are no longer the politically and economically dominant group; they take orders rather than give them, and they search for jobs instead of providing them. As immigrants they have to cope with unfamiliar laws and customs. England is a dramatic contrast to their original situation.

The social and political repercussions of these Sikh migrations have tended to create problems in both India and Britain. Authorities of both governments are concerned and affected by the affairs of these people, and governmental administrators have to develop appropriate policies to deal with present and future situations created by these sojourners. This monograph is a descriptive and analytical portrayal of these proud Sikh

Jats whose behaviour and problems have had and will very likely continue to have far-reaching consequences for both countries.

Thus, this study presents an historical profile of the Gravesend immigrant community which will be interesting and informative to the non-professional as well as to social scientists. This study describes how the Sikh Jats have sought to cope with their new situation and adjust to the problems created by both their host and home societies. In the adaptation process for many of the immigrants, there is a three-way interaction among the sending, receiving and migrant communities. Accordingly, this work presents a narrative of these Asians, starting with the emigration process in the Punjab and continuing with a study of their lives in British society. The first three chapters describe the people studied, explain their cultural values, their home situation, and the factors that led to emigration. Their experience in Britain, set forth in the later chapters, falls naturally into three sections: beginning years (1947–59), massive influx (1960–2), and the settlement period (1963–71). The Epilogue (a fourth period) updates the circumstances in Gravesend (1978) and sets forth the problems faced by second-generation immigrants, for these are increasing in gravity as the 1980s approach.

Many migrant groups seek to maintain a sense of identity and separateness from their host community. The Sikhs in England are no exception. This study, however, shows how the sending and receiving societies influence the maintenance or demise of social boundaries between these sojourners in England and other communities.

The initial data for this work was obtained in 1970–1. My family and I lived and participated in the social life of the Gravesend Indian community for seven months. The time in England was followed by a six-month stay in Jandiali, a sending village in Punjab, India. A follow-up study of both communities was undertaken in 1978. Both my wife and I have an intimate knowledge of Indian culture and speak the Punjabi language. This enabled us to gain acceptance and facilitated effective communication. Much of the actual data gained by our experience is presented to the reader, who can thus evaluate the basis from which abstractions and conclusions are reached.

The illustrations and cases used are representative of immigrant situations. As a result, numerous South Asians will be able to identify with the narratives presented, even though actual identities have been disguised. By using individual experiences to develop generalities, it is hoped that the reader will have a greater understanding, both emotional and theoretical, of why these immigrants left their homes in the Punjab, and why the situation has become so strained in contemporary Britain for all concerned.

August 1979   A. W. H.

ACKNOWLEDGEMENTS

A study like this is never accomplished alone; it is a group project which results in the author receiving the credit. Unfortunately, if all those deserving recognition were to be named, the study itself would not have sufficient space to set forth proper acknowledgements. Thus, I hope that a general expression of gratitude will be accepted by the numerous people who have offered hospitality and time to answer my many queries. Special thanks, however, must be given to Dr Robert McKinley, Professor Hugh Tinker, Dr William T. Ross, Professor André Béteille, Professor Baljit Singh and the Oxford University Press, Delhi, who have kindly read and offered their valuable comments on this manuscript. In Gravesend, Mr Charles Revis (then Community Relations Officer), Mr Jagdev Singh Sandu, Mr G. B. S. Wasu, Mr Kirpal Singh Uppal, Masterji Atwall, Dr G. V. W. Ellis, Mr Jai Singh, Mr Bahadur Singh Randhawa, Mr Charan Singh and Mrs Jagira Kaur Goodwin and her family for their patience in providing assistance.

In India, I am indebted especially to Professor M. S. A. Rao of Delhi University, Dr A. R. Mehta, Mr and Mrs Mahesh Sarin, and Mr and Mrs Gautam Singh, who provided insight into Indian culture. In Jandiali, Mr Darshan Singh Birring, Mr Sadhu Singh, Mr Hardial Singh, Mr Ajit Singh Lyall and Mr Sital Singh Birring all provided time, information, and hospitality.

Editorial help was provided by Toni Gross, Kate Williams, Dr Jack C. Plano, and my wife, Usha, who tirelessly laboured over this manuscript, offering suggestions and help. Mrs Jan Duszynski typed the manuscript. I must, however, take full responsibility for any errors or inadequacies.

This study was made possible by financial assistance from the Institute of Race Relations, London; the Asian Studies Center of Michigan State University; and a National Defense Foreign Language Fellowship. A follow-up project was sponsored by a Fulbright Hayes Faculty Research Grant.

CHAPTER I

THE PEOPLE STUDIED: PUNJABIS, SIKHS AND JATS

Misconceptions of migrant behaviour

Race relations and immigration to England are two topics of paramount concern in both Great Britain and India. Articles in newspapers of both countries frequently report and give prominence to ethnic clashes, alien behaviour, or pronouncements on policies concerning minorities. Terms like 'coloureds', 'Sikhs', 'Bangladeshis', and 'Pakistanis' frequently appear in print and many a conversation. The Punjabi Sikh Jats (i.e. a caste group, predominantly farmers, who live in the Indian state of Punjab) are only one category of those who have migrated to Britain, but they are prominent, both because of their appearance and numbers. The turban and beard of the man, along with the *salwar-kameez* of the woman, make them noticeable. These dress distinctions, plus their banding together in communities where their rural culture is transplanted, make them appear more numerous than they actually may be. An Englishman walking through their residential area may feel like a foreigner in his own country and fear that the Asians are taking over his homeland. Southall is one such place and is appropriately called '*Chota* Punjab', meaning 'Little Punjab'.

An understanding of these immigrants from Punjab is not only important for the social scientist but also for the layman who has to deal with them. The average Englishman and Indian needs information concerning these new arrivals so he can intelligently evaluate stories, pronouncements and policies that are continually reported. The recent influx of migrants, along with available information concerning their sending situation, also provides an opportunity for the social scientist to examine migrant behaviour within a three-way interaction process of the sending, receiving, and transient communities. Therefore this work focuses on studying Punjabi Sikh Jat adaptive behaviour in England. A secondary consideration is given to the reciprocal influence of the sojourners on both the British and Indian communities with which they interact.

Generalizations about the Punjabi Sikh Jat migrants of this study who originate from the villages are not necessarily applicable to other South Asians or immigrants. Punjabis from Delhi and other urban Indian centres often fail to understand their village counterparts. In fact, those from the cities often evaluate the peasant by their own ethnocentric ideas and are frequently embarrassed by rural behaviour. The villagers also have their biases and may not accept metropolitan behaviour or clothing, such as a sari, as Indian or proper. Yet there is a tendency in Britain to treat all immigrant communities, especially South Asians, as a single category. But, even within India, there is tremendous cultural disparity between different groups; and generalizations about one social unit may not be applicable to another, despite both hailing from the same subcontinent. The emphasis of this study is on the Punjabi Sikh Jats of rural Punjab who migrated to England and comprise about 60 per cent of the Indian immigrant population in that country.[1]

Group distinctions

For a fuller understanding of the people of this treatise, each term, 'Punjabi', 'Sikh', and 'Jat', is initially examined as a category in itself, for each encompasses a wider range of people than is considered in this work. Generally, however, these terms will be used interchangeably in this study and refer only to the more precise category of Sikh villagers who have emigrated from rural Punjab to the United Kingdom.

Punjab (Figure 1), the land of five rivers, lies in the northwestern sector of the South Asian continent and is divided by the boundaries of India and Pakistan. This geographical area contains a wide range of people—Sikhs, Hindus, and Muslims —all of whom go under the generic 'Punjabi'. As a result, Indians, Pakistanis, and other people from geographical Punjab (Figure 1) consider themselves Punjabis. Like some other groups, the Sikhs and Jats of this study are primarily Punjabis for they claim Punjab as their homeland and share with other Punjabis a common language (Punjabi), homeland (Punjab), distinctive dress (salwar-kameez for women), history, family pattern, art, and value system. Consequently, even though the locution 'Punjabi' refers to a much wider range of people than is focused on in this study, this label will be used interchangeably with 'Sikh' and 'Jat' to refer to the people on which this work concentrates.

The Sikhs are a religious community claiming geographical Punjab (Figure 1) as their homeland. Since Guru Nanak (1469–1539) founded the sect, they have suffered from and defended themselves against persecution. This continual oppression and the massive conversion of Jats to Sikhism under Guru Arjun Dev (1563–1606) contributed to the religious community being transformed from a peaceful group, attempting to unify Islam and Hinduism, into an aggressive, militaristic, soldier-saint brotherhood known as the *Khalsa*.

The Sikhs are very noticeable because of their distinctive symbols: cohesiveness, strong communal pride, easy adaptability to new and different situations and martial spirit. All of these qualities are prominent among the Sikhs in England. Although neatly ordered under a turban, uncut hair (*kes*) is their most distinctive symbol; others include an iron bracelet on the right wrist (*karha*), a sword (*kirpan*), a comb in the hair (*kangha*), and specially designed undershorts (*kachha*). These five K's, as they are called, communicate the soldier-saint ideal of this religious community.

For Sikhs in both India and England, their hair is the most controversial symbol. Many individuals who claim membership in the khalsa find it expedient to shave. Villagers migrating to England with unshorn locks often cut them to gain employment. Sikh boys with their braids or topknots often experience humiliation in British schools, for long hair does not have the same connotations of manliness and sainthood in the West as it does in the East. Most Sikhs are taught to consider their unshorn hair as a symbol of strength; therefore shaving makes them feel less-of-a-man. However, to prove one's worth the importance of a well-paid job far outweighs feelings of male potency. Debate among Sikhs, both in the migrant community and in India, continues as to whether a Sikh with shorn tresses

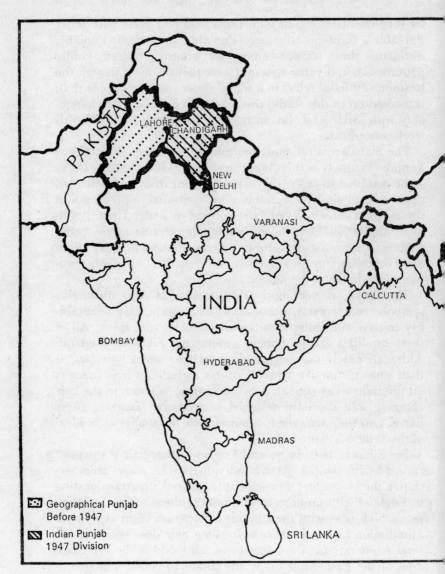

Figure 1. Location of Punjab

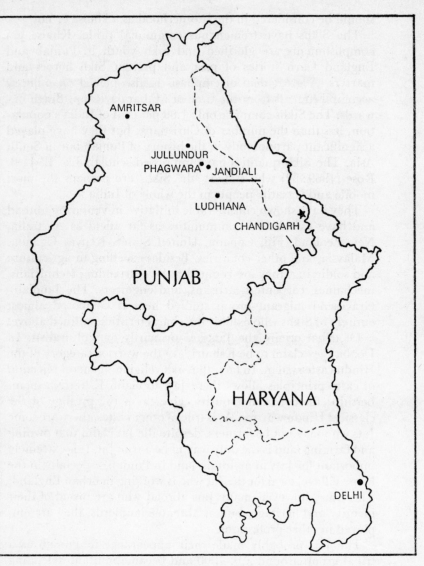

Figure 2. Location of Jandiali

should be considered in the brotherhood as a khalsa or not.

The Sikhs have tremendous communal pride. Khalsa accomplishments are glorified and Sikh youth in Punjab and England learn stories of past and present Sikh heroes and martyrs. A great deal of emphasis is also placed on military accomplishments from the time of Maharaja Ranjit Singh onwards. The Sikhs comprise only 1.89 per cent of India's population, less than the number of Christians; but they have played a significant part not only in the history of Punjab but in South Asia. The Sikh qualities have impressed scholars like E. J. B. Rose (1969: 52) who stated: 'the Sikhs are perhaps the most mobile and versatile people in the whole of India'.

They have shown considerable initiative in venturing abroad and have established communities as far afield as Australia, New Zealand, Fiji, Canada, United States, Kenya, Uganda, Malaysia, and other countries. Besides excelling in agriculture and soldiering, they are reputed to be outstanding technicians, mechanics, carpenters, artisans, and engineers. The Jandiali–Gravesend migrant group studied here is composed almost entirely of Sikhs who exhibit the characteristics outlined above. Of tribal origin, the Jats are primarily agriculturalists. In Doaba they claim to be Kshatriyas,[2] the warrior category of the Hindu caste system. In fact, the Sikh religion's general rejection of caste principles allows these Jats to claim Kshatriya membership; for deeds, not purity, give them the prestige of the classical Hindu warrior. As is true of other castes, there are some Jats who may not be farmers, despite the Jat claim that owning and farming land is the only way to be a true Jat. It is extremely important for Jats to maintain land in Punjab, especially in the home village, even for the Jat who is working in urban England. There are, however, many Jats abroad who are proud of their identity and heritage, but, as absentee landlords, they are employed in other professions.

The Jats probably made their appearance in Punjab as a tribal group around A.D. 1000 and became militant defending themselves against numerous invasions. Under Guru Arjun Dev, many Jats embraced Sikhism and contributed to the development of the martial valour of that religion. Present-day Jats are by far the dominant group amongst the Sikhs. In fact, when Sikh Jat culture is studied, it is almost impossible to separate the 'Sikh' from the 'Jat', as their goals and values are tightly intertwined. However, Jats are considered a caste and ethnic category and not a religious group; therefore, they can be Muslim, Hindu, or Sikh. The Jats of this study, however, are primarily Sikhs.

The Jats have been agriculturalists, a very able, proud, independent, and self-reliant people. Their mode of government has been the traditional panchayat in which five elders are elected as a ruling group to legislate, administrate, and adjudicate. Until recently,

every Jat village was a small republic made up of people of kindred blood who were as conscious of absolute equality between themselves as they were aware of their superiority over men of other castes. . . . The relationship of a Jat village with the state was that of a semi-autonomous unit paying a fixed sum of revenue (Singh, Khushwant 1963:15).

This separateness from their government and uniting against what they perceive as outside opposition is a trait of today's Jat immigrants in England. As in the village, they may have internal conflict, but they converge when an external threat appears.

In Punjab villages, Jats often dominate numerically, politically and economically, and are extremely proud of their heritage, thus carrying an aura of superiority about them. They demand strict adherence to their cultural norms from fellow members and rigidly enforce these customs on their children, especially the girls. This enforcement of Jat culture is also characteristic among their community abroad. There are other caste groups among the Jandiali–Gravesend migrant group, but here too, the Jats are most numerous and have strong influence in the Indian community affairs of Gravesend.

Punjab's history is turbulent due to its strategic location on the invasion route into India. This area has continually been the battlefield for encroachers whose cultural influence, especially Muslim, has played a significant role in the development of its society and culture. Many years of alien rule instilled in the villagers a view that governmental bureaucrats are not to be trusted[3]—a view the Jat immigrants have carried with them to England. Freedom from British rule briefly calmed the turbulence of this area. But the creation of Pakistan in 1947 resulted in riots, bloodshed and one of history's great human migrations—Sikhs and Hindus going east and Muslims fleeing west. These unsettled conditions have helped create a versatile and mobile community which is not rigidly bound by customs nor traditions—they are flexible and willing to move or adopt new ideas to suit their purpose.

To accommodate Sikh demands, East Punjab in India was further divided in 1966 to create the Hindi-speaking state of Haryana and the Punjabi-speaking state of Punjab.[4] In this study, the term 'Punjab' will mostly refer to this newly created unit outlined in Figure 2. Before the 1947 partition, the Sikhs comprised about 13 per cent of the undivided Punjab's population; they now claim 55 per cent in the present state.

The present creation of the Indian government labelled 'Punjab', India (Figure 2) is a fertile region with the Beas and Sutlej rivers watering this 50,376 square kilometre area which supports a population of 13,551,060. It is often called the 'California', 'bread basket', 'granary' or 'Canada' of India. Such titles are well deserved, for Punjab has only 2.6 per cent of the total net sown area of the country; yet it produces 7 per cent of India's total food grains. Punjab also leads all other Indian states in boasting the highest per capita income (Rs 1482), highest percentage of irrigated area (71 per cent), highest agricultural production (food grains, especially wheat, are in surplus), highest number of tractors, highest milk yield, highest life expectancy, highest wages for agricultural labourers and largest number of roads.

Between the Beas and Sutlej rivers lies a rich, fertile Doaba (land between two tributaries) which comprises the districts of Jullundur, Kapurthala and Hoshiarpur.[5] This general area is the origin of most of the Punjabi immigrants to England. It is a comparatively rich countryside dotted with tube-wells spurting life-giving water and transforming a potentially barren area into rich agricultural land.

Since Punjab is a comparatively prosperous region, the question of motivation for emigration is an interesting one. Economic conditions and land pressure are indeed major inducements for leaving—residence in Britain provides access to a quantity and quality of resources often unavailable to these people in their villages. Chapter III, however, will show that non-economic factors have also played a role in motivating Sikh emigration from Punjab. Also, Sikh Jats have traditionally been a peripatetic group with exaggerated tales of glory and excitement abroad encouraging others to follow. Economic reasons thus have proved to be only one of many criteria for these peoples' decisions to emigrate.

In conclusion, it can be stated that the Sikh Jats from Punjabi villages who have migrated to Britain are a cohesive, aggressive community which is mobile, flexible and proud. They are respected by outsiders and suggest a heritage which gives them a high opinion of their traditions and beliefs. Their accomplishments are numerous. How such a people deal with the situation in England will be a major concern in this study.

CHAPTER II

THE CULTURAL CONTEXT

Honour–Shame

When reporting and analysing migrant behaviour, it is essential to consider the culturally determined yet subjective views of the people themselves. The cultural notion of honour or *izzat*, along with related concepts, greatly colours the Punjabi migrant's attitudes and perceptions of his experience in England and are worth considering here.

Generally among this group, honour, like reputation, can be enhanced in many ways; it is to be protected and regained when lost. The migrant situation, which engenders thoughts of a fresh start, sensitizes the sojourner to his cultural concept of honour, especially whilst maintaining close communication with his home village and others from his area of origin. To understand the effect of prestige considerations on Jat actions in Britain, it is necessary to comprehend their system of evaluating one another and its behavioural ramifications. Peristiany (1966) has encountered like issues among certain Mediterranean cultures where there appears to be a definite similarity between the Punjabi concept of izzat and the 'honour–shame' concept.

As set forth by Peristiany (1966:12), 'honour' and 'shame' are two polar extremes of representative behaviour in certain cultures. Honour is an extremely favourable appraisal placed by the society on individuals, families, or groups when their behaviour is in accordance with culturally preferred standards. The evaluative criteria are usually an ideal type of action which is considered representative or exemplary for the community. There is, however, an aggressive side to the honour complex as it also implies a credibility of promises and threats and a possessiveness of individual and familial rights, including rights of property, women, and social privileges. Possessiveness regarding rights over women is especially crucial to such systems, because tight control over females of one's own group directly influences others who seek these women in marriage. Honourable behaviour may also involve taking someone else's property, life, or honour, while retaining one's own credibility. Basically, honour requires obtaining and maintaining respect not only for oneself but for the whole group.

Shame, on the other hand, is the public rejection of one's performance and, therefore, results in disrepute. For example, a Jat daughter who develops a reputation for looseness brings shame upon herself and her whole family. In rare cases, parents may have an erring daughter killed to restore kin honour.[1] For social evaluation, honour and shame provide an actor with criteria to estimate his own public worth. It is this aspect which helps explain why the notion of honour carries great force as a source of social motivation and as a mechanism of social control.

In Gravesend the Punjabis are deeply concerned about their izzat or *mann*[2] as evaluated by three different audiences: (1) villagers in Punjab, (2) Punjabis in England, and (3) the English host community. The first two categories have the strongest influence on their behaviour but it is interesting to note how the Punjabis have projected their own culture onto the host group. According to their self-assessment of izzat, esteem in the eyes of others is not dependent upon another group sharing a similar concept. Izzat is so entrenched in Sikh Jat culture that an appreciation of it can be projected on to outsiders. Both in England and India, Punjabis are concerned that they and their fellows exemplify honourable behaviour. In effect, this projection of their own values on the British serves primarily to rally their own sense of superiority over the host population.

An individual's izzat is especially vulnerable as it is considered largely in the context of group membership. A Punjabi may possess izzat but the unbecoming and shameful behaviour of his children can certainly detract from his honour and place him under censure for not enforcing his high principles on his offspring. Therefore personal prestige is subordinated to the communal evaluation of his group, whether it be family, *biradari*, or other unit. A son may have to subordinate his desire to venture into a lucrative business if his father feels that it would detract from the family's reputation. Supporting the group's izzat is of prime importance for Punjabis, and it is within the

context of izzat and other related precepts that Punjabis evaluate their behaviour and the actions of outsiders.

The eight other related concepts that influence Punjabi
behaviour in their own right are: *muhabbat* (brotherly love),
khidmat (hospitality), *seva* (service to others), caste, *robh* (power),
jaidad (wealth), *zamindari* (land ownership) and *pirhi* (generation).

Muhabbat is deep affection and loyalty of one person for
another. This love or brotherliness can be symbolized in many
ways. One such method is exchanging turbans and pledging
brotherhood and *muhabbat* unto death. Customarily this love is
so binding that the two will trust each other with their lives.

This *muhabbat* is also manifested through lending money in
time of need without expecting return, aiding in sickness and
bereavement, and providing food and shelter for an indefinite
period. *Muhabbat* is more than a social obligation: it is standing
by another person or family because of heart-felt and deep
emotional attachment. It is a relationship based on depth of
affection and not on obligation or social pressure. Such relationships are often established and relied upon by the Punjabis
in England.

Khidmat refers to the Punjabi concept of hospitality. In England, there are numerous tales of Punjabi émigré arriving with
a meagre three pounds[3] in their pockets being taken in by Sikh
Jats who not only provided food and shelter for an indefinite
period but helped the newcomer to find a job. Many testimonies
bear witness to the fact that their hosts expected or demanded
nothing except a bond of mutual friendship. Punjabi culture is
one where hospitality is continually offered.

Seva or service is performed for others, whether it be for an
individual or the community in general. In analytical terms,
it is the practice of general reciprocity set forth by Sahlins
(1965:147), where one provides help or a gift without expecting
return; it is the sustained one-way flow of goods and services.
For the Punjabi, credit for *seva* varies with the circumstances.
The following two extreme examples will illustrate the concept:

Once, they say, a thief came in at the dead of night, hounded by the
police. Kabir quietly put him alongside his own daughter and asked
him to go to sleep. The police came and saw no stranger there. Here
was Kabir, there his son, there his wife and yonder his daughter and

his son-in-law! This was one small act of a truly spiritual person. (Singh, Puran n.d.:23)

Kabir was not concerned with whether the man was guilty of committing the crime but that the situation required help or service to an individual. A similar point is further exemplified in more recent writings as the following extract from Khushwant Singh's (1956:37) *Train to Pakistan* shows:

For them [the Sikh villagers] truth, honour, financial integrity were 'all right', but these were placed lower down the scale of values than being true to one's self, to one's friends and fellow villagers. For friends, you could lie in court or cheat, and no one would blame you . . . everyone in the village was a relation and loyalty to the village was the supreme test. . . . If Jugga had done the same thing [committed murder] in the neighbouring village, Meet Singh [the village Sikh priest] would gladly have appeared in his defence and sworn on the Holy Granth that Jugga had been praying in the gurdwara at the time of the murder.

Seva for the migrants in Britain takes on many forms; working for the gurdwara (the Sikh place of worship), helping the community in England, or financing projects in the home village are but a few ways of doing so.

Caste concepts of separation, inequality and hereditary specialization with the ranking of behaviour along the purity–pollution continuum are present in Punjabi life. The Sikh bond with Hinduism has never been severed in spite of the Sikh gurus rejecting caste.

The influence of the caste system for Punjabi migrants generally takes the form of feeling a sense of Jat superiority towards their hosts—in caste ideology, even the lowest caste Indians are ranked above the westerners. The émigré outwardly associates with and respects his British host, whereas inwardly he evaluates certain western cultural traits as polluting, defiling, and immoral. Dating, janitorial work, and sitting in one's bath water are but a few defiling western traits.

Given the ethnic and class context of the Punjabi migrants, the South Asian heritage of caste has been used to construct a negative stereotype of the British. But, with respect to his own behaviour, the Jat may be less strict, especially with regard to male actions. Punjabis in England want to insure that their village counterparts regard them as uncorrupted by English ways.[4] Therefore, outwardly, the Jats in Gravesend keep up a semblance of strictness and adherence to caste dictates in order to receive a favourable evaluation for izzat considerations.

Robh, or power, is another goal sought after by Sikh Jats. Generally in Indian society a powerful person is 'one who sees to the welfare of many kinsmen' (Mandelbaum 1972:156). But for the Sikh Jats, benefits to others is not necessarily limited to kinsmen. Hence an individual's *robh* is measured by the amount of aid bestowed on others and the numbers of his following. If a person does not look after his supporters, he is weak, regardless of the resources at his disposal. A *robhdar* Jat must have followers to defend himself during a time of challenge, otherwise he is deemed impotent. Therefore Punjabi migrants associate closely with kinsmen and loyal village-mates. Patronage can be acquired also by ready assistance to others, like helping fellow village-mates settle in Britain, coping with the English bureaucracy and effectively dealing with extortioners. Obtaining and using power properly helps gain prestige.

Jaidad, or wealth, is an end in itself, or a means to gain and maintain izzat. A person or family is generally evaluated by the amount of service or patronage bestowed. A very rich family, without too much sacrifice, can readily support community approved goals. Because they give more than others, their service is rated higher than a competitor who may be giving all that he has. *Jaidad* often has additional advantages other than monetary. A wealthy family normally has political, financial and business contacts that can benefit fellow villagers or friends. These acquaintances may be more valuable than monetary transactions. Unquestionably, then, wealth is a resource for enhancing and acquiring prestige.

Jaidad in and of itself is often displayed in the gold jewelry worn by the womenfolk, thus demonstrating their riches and respectability. In the village of Jandiali, large houses are built by emigrants to show off their acquired wealth, though they may never live in these houses. Huge dowries are given to the girls to suggest that they come from a wealthy family; with the corollary of the bride having a better chance to *robh* in her new abode.

In the late 1950s and early 1960s, to be an 'England returnee' bequeathed dignity to a person and his family. According to the belief of many villagers, returnees are always rich and successful. For a person or family with no hope of social mobility in the village, going to England is a suitable route to follow. Money for service to the village will be available and the family will profit by having an 'England returnee' in their midst.

Zamindari or owning land are emulative roles for the village Jats. An émigré may work in a factory, own a store, or engage in other kinds of lucrative labour, but he generally feels inadequate or unfulfilled if he is not a zamindar. In Jat culture, owning acreage is essential for self-respect and is a source of power and prestige. A Jat will resist disposing of his land which also symbolizes royalty and is closely linked with power over other men. The Jat's 'self-definition of manliness includes an ability with live-stock and skill in farming' (Kessinger 1974:103); thus, a good farmer is greatly admired by the Jats.

Zamindari aspirations result in many Jat immigrants buying land whether or not they themselves will ever till it. It is a secure basis for attaining *robh*, *jaidad*, financial security and 'roots' for himself and his family.

Pirhi literally means generation and refers to the prestige that has accrued to a family through its history. A family may originate from a good *pirhi* or bad *pirhi*, that is, an individual may come from a good or bad family. The Jats in England generally look up to members of high *pirhi* families for leadership. An individual's behaviour may not be up to expectations, but being from a high *pirhi* family is to his credit. Punjabi immigrants in Gravesend from low *pirhi* families can overcome their low heritage by providing brokerage services and/or *seva* to others. They use their resources to help village projects, kin, and friends in Punjab. Thus for many, emigration from Jandiali is an acceptable means to overcome the stigma of being from a low *pirhi* family.

The Punjabi immigrants to Gravesend come from a rural society with a general cultural goal of obtaining and enhancing their izzat. However, there are numerous associated goals that help enhance prestige or are ends in themselves. The following section will illustrate how cultural concepts affect migrant behaviour and perceptions.

Culture in action

In the situation of Punjabi villagers, the variables involved in social evaluation are great. The following cases[5] and subsequent explanations are presented to illustrate in reality some of the concepts discussed:

Sajan Singh,[6] a Punjabi villager, is considered an honest and devout Sikh Jat who is very highly respected for his integrity. His family was poor, but his father and brother emigrated to England and left Sajan Singh behind to maintain the family farm. Along with that joint property, Sajan Singh was left responsible for the land of other village-mates who had gone to England and entrusted their small holdings to him. In all, he now farms forty acres (although only seven acres belong to him), has a tractor and owns tube-wells.

Sajan Singh has been successful in establishing contacts and has helped many families migrate to England. He is the spokesman for his less affluent village-mates and the lower castes like the Ramgardiahs, Jheers, Chamars, and other Jats. By helping these people he has unanimously become their *Sarpanch* (head of the ruling village council) although the actual title belongs to the wealthiest man in the district.

Whenever any villager or émigré needs help to look after a relative, to handle money in Punjab, care for land, or promote a village project, they approach Sajan Singh, being certain that it will be satisfactorily and expediently taken care of.

Not only is Sajan Singh a humble man, but he is proud of his humility.[7] Although a Jat does not ask for anything in return for his help, it is proper for him to expect and receive recognition for it. When I discovered that Sajan Singh was considered a Sarpanch by some I asked him why he had not said anything. Sajan proudly replied, 'I am a humble man.' When a *Nahang* tried to convert Sajan Singh to his sect, Sajan argued, 'Since all paths lead to God and I am a good and righteous man, I will be with God, therefore, why should I become a *Nahang*?' This was an impressive argument that could not be countered.

Sajan Singh had one serious problem, however. He was very anxious to send his son abroad because the lad was lazy and an alcoholic, hence, a potential threat to family honour. Sajan's wife stated that they wanted the son in England where he could be successful before the whole village started to point a finger at Sajan Singh indicating that, 'He who helps everyone else, is incapable of helping his own son', thus damaging family izzat. 'After all, there are younger daughters and nieces in the family who are of marriageable age', she explained.

Sajan Singh is a man who actually owns seven acres of land, yet by his own honesty and help from relatives abroad, he has developed certain resources to gain the title of unofficial head-man for about half the village. There are others with more wealth than Sajan Singh, but they do not use their resources as wisely in communal service as he does. Originally he was a weak and poor man who gained izzat by serving others, that is, by establishing a relationship of general reciprocity with a number of his village-mates. The reward for his help is their support and loyalty to him, making him a strong man with the right to manage some of their resources. As an able and trusted steward, he has both influence and respect.

Sajan Singh's son may be his father's downfall and ruin among the kin group. If the son is not moulded into a responsible individual, according to the villagers, most of what Sajan Singh has worked for in his life will be in vain. Sajan Singh will be evaluated harshly by his village-mates for spending his time on others for self-enhancement at the cost of his own family—all members of a family are affected by the behaviour of one individual member. The plan to send the young lad to England has possibilities because firstly, being put in an environment of regimentation and hard work, he will be forced to develop some responsibility. Secondly, he can redeem himself by sending money back to the village, and finally, even if his behaviour continues to be irresponsible in England, the family can claim that it is a vicious and untrue rumour. The village may know differently, but at least there will be a semblance of doubt, whereas if the son stays on in the village his failings will be apparent to all the villagers. In other words, his case exemplifies how a family can effectively use migration as a means of managing their public image.

The eighty-year-old mother of a prominent businessman demonstrated such senile behaviour as walking into the living room without clothes and even relieving herself on the living room rug. As this was harmful to his business, he placed the elderly lady in a home for such people, where she died about a year later. The son and his wife were severely condemned by the community for not fulfilling their obligations to the elderly mother who had given him birth, loved and cared for him throughout his childhood, and sacrificed herself for her children. Because of their selfishness, they and their progeny had lost her blessings.

Also, the business had to be moved, for any son who treated his mother in such a manner was not patronized by the community. The izzat of the family was severely damaged in the eyes of the community.

Service within the kin group is as important, if not more so, than service to outsiders. These cases show that concern of consanguines is very important in gaining a high evaluation. If family members are loyal and helpful to one another, they are considered an *izzatwali* family, a family with high honour.

Notice also that internal family affairs are the concern of the whole community. If an individual does not behave properly toward his own parents, not only is family prestige diminished, but the community may, in some cases, take steps to correct the situation. All members of the community are responsible for the actions of their fellow members. Placing purely internal affairs within the sole province of the family or group is not a Sikh cultural trait.

Mahesh Singh, the oldest son in the family, went to England, became a doctor, and then returned to Punjab. Mahesh was competent and rose in the government health service. Pal, the younger brother, however, behaved improperly. He would not give his wife money to buy food, nor would he give money for his children's clothes. Pal did not keep a steady job, and when he did receive money, he would squander it on drink. Although he was not rich, Mahesh provided Pal's wife with money for food and clothes. He paid a local tailor to teach Pal a trade and paid for a shop so that Pal would start a business. After many years, Pal became reasonably responsible, and due to Mahesh's efforts family izzat was maintained and upheld.

One family member's behaviour affects the whole kin group. It was Mahesh's responsibility as an older brother to assure the maintenance of family honour, therefore he helped and watched over his younger brother. The irresponsibility had to be controlled, not simply disowned. Had the older brother neglected his duty, or failed, his family would have lost their high izzat in the eyes of the community.

Gopal Singh is presently the Sarpanch of his village. His father before him held the position and his grandfather before that. His family is wealthy, owning hundreds of acres of land, not all of which is in the home village. Whenever there is a problem or need for the village or its members, people go to Gopal Singh. Nothing is too big or too small for his assistance. If the local factory needs money, they go to Gopal Singh, who arranges a loan from the local bank. He is the most highly respected man in the village, and it is likely that his young son, who now handles many of his elderly father's affairs, will follow in his steps. Gopal Singh's son emigrated to Canada and is training to be a doctor. His brother is a postal official in the nearby town of Phagwara. Unfortunately, their sister, Jagir Kaur, had a bad marriage. Immediately after the ceremony the groom sent her home claiming she was very ugly. Gopal's family, however, claims that the groom is a homosexual. In either case, Gopal's sister has redeemed herself as the local school teacher and pledged herself to a life of service to the girls in the village. She is recognized as a fine, loving teacher and is highly respected.

Gopal Singh's family is of very high izzat and in some respects represents an ideal family of high honour. Traditionally, the family had produced leaders. Gopal Singh uses his wealth and land in performing the highest services for the village. He is strong because of the following he attracts. Furthermore, his brother and son hold good positions which greatly contribute to the honour of the family. Having another son who can become a doctor abroad also enhances the father's position in the eyes of his rural community. Both tradition and the behaviour of kinsmen enhance Gopal Singh's family's prestige, and Gopal Singh, in turn, supports his family by his impeccable behaviour. All are affected by the actions of each group member.

Having a sister rejected by a groom was a blow to family honour, for a woman can damage the family name more easily than a man. Gopal's sister redeemed her izzat and that of her family by immersing herself in service to the village.

Maintaining group and individual esteem as evaluated by one's community is a guiding principle among rural Punjabis in England. And although the presentation here is by no means exhaustive, it gives the reader an idea of the cultural framework in which the rural Punjabis in England evaluate themselves and their hosts. With these values and concepts in mind, the story of these immigrants will now be told.

CHAPTER III

EMIGRATION STARTS

Punjabis in general

Punjabis consider themselves a modern and international people. As one villager expressed it, 'Potatoes and Punjabis are found all over the world!' There is an oft-repeated joke in Punjab that when Neil Armstrong landed on the moon, a Sikh taxi driver tapped him on the shoulder and asked, 'Taxi, Sahib?' Another variation states that during the above incident, a Jat ploughing the ground passed the astronaut!

Migration is part of the Punjabi heritage. Punjabis were originally in mobile bands, whose contact with the outside world had been considerable due to their location on the East–West trade route. The import of European officers to train Maharaja Ranjit Singh's army further exposed these people to western culture. After the British established control of the region, many were exported due to the indentured labour system and the development of Canal Colonies.

Sikh *jawans* (soldiers) were used in the British army, thus contributing to the affinity Punjabis felt towards their rulers. In the military under British rule, there developed a

sympathy, a mutual respect, a trust between British officer and Sikh. It was something personal, that was to blossom between one man and another, or between one man and a regiment or half a district, intermittently, here and there until Independence (Mason 1974: 230).

Serving in the English army in both World Wars brought Sikhs into further close contact with Britain.

During the early twentieth-century, Bhatras, a *biradari* in the Jullundur Doab, were brought from their villages to Bombay, taught a smattering of English, and shipped to London to sell trinkets. In the 1920s, these peddlers, many of whom were Sikh, were found displaying their wares in Hyde Park, Oxford Circus, and eventually establishing businesses in East London. England was also the educational centre for the British Empire, and Punjabis, like other subjects, turned to England for higher education. In the early years, few students settled abroad, and many returned home.

All was not harmony between the Punjabis and the English. Prosperity in the Punjab was shortlived and by the early twentieth century Anglo-Punjabi relations began to deteriorate. The Ghadr party, which was formed to liberate Punjab, failed and by World War II became dormant. Before 1940, resources had been sufficiently taxed and Punjabis were looking for new opportunities which took some to England for economic enhancement.

Post-World War II saw England with about 5,000 Indians. Many times that number were in East Africa. Sikh communities had been established in Burma, Malaya, Singapore, Thailand, Cambodia, the Philippines, China, the United States, and Canada. Besides those few Punjabis already in England, ex-soldiers, students, professionals, businessmen, and jawans helped fellow Punjabis migrate. For the villagers, jawans and Bhatras were the most likely source of aid.

Families pooled resources to send a capable member abroad. He would in turn help others. Information spread as wives wrote to their villages describing England as the land of opportunity. Newspaper articles supporting this view appeared in all languages. Those left destitute by the 1947 partition of India looked to England for a fresh start. Rose (1969:70) interestingly notes that the refugees from West Punjab (Pakistan) generally did not emigrate until their land claims were settled and they had obtained their compensation.

Rose (1969:70–3) also rightly points out that travel agents were responsible for the mass exodus to England, but that the tight social networks played a greater part in communicating the advantages of going 'phoren'.[1] The main influx came in the early 1960s with the threat and passage of restrictive legislation for immigration to Britain. Under that impetus, many emigrated who otherwise may not have left Punjab. This legislation prompted the 1962 influx of Punjabi women, thus increasing the female element well above the initial 4 per cent. The presence of children gave even greater permanency to the Punjabi community in England.

The Doaba region of Punjab that has sent most of the Sikh

Jat migrants to England is the setting for Jandiali, one small village which has been the home for many emigrants. Jandiali is important to report on because of the fact that the communications networks with the home villagers has affected and still affects behaviour in England. This is because the reference group of imitation for most of the Sikh Jats in the United Kingdom is their village of origin. Of course it must be kept in mind that villages vary in this region. There are Brahmin-dominated villages or villages where Ramgardiahs are most numerous and the religion may be Hindu or Sikh. However, Jandiali is a Sikh village inhabited predominantly by Jats.

Including emigrants, Jandiali's population of 1,608 (see Appendix A) has 309 low-caste people living in Chamali and a total of 830 Jats. Ramgardiahs, Jheers, Brahmins, Ramdasis, Lohars, Kumhars, Sunyars, Marasis, and Bhangis constitute the remainder of the populace. The few Hindu families in the village are those of the Brahmins, Sunyars, and Adharmis.

Of Jandiali's 515 emigrants, 402 are in England, others reside in parts of northern and central India, and a few are scattered abroad, mainly in New Zealand, Australia, Canada, and the Philippines. Most Jandialian émigrés are young males, which explains the noticeable lack of people (especially men) between the ages of twenty and forty in the village. Virtually every Jat household in this village claims at least one or more member overseas, mostly in England.

Of its 646 acres of land, 555 are irrigated primarily by tube-wells (most of which were financed by emigrant money); only one or two Persian wheels are still being used. Jandialians also control approximately 215 acres of land in neighbouring villages and over 1,000 acres in Rajasthan and U.P.

Jandialians go 'phoren'

The emigration of Jandialians to the United States and Canada started when a Chamar, Ganda Singh, who had been a sweeper on the Indian Railways, became involved with the Ghadr Party. Before World War II, the Ghadrs sponsored his emigration to train him as a local insurgent. He was to help promote an uprising in Punjab, but he ended in Edinburgh, where he had a small business in cloth. When World War II broke out, Ganda Singh feared being drafted into the British Armed Forces so he returned to Jandiali via the United States, working for his passage home. Although this man, ninety years old at the time of the study, had a comfortable home in Chamali, indicating that he must have brought back considerable savings, he continued to work as a field hand during harvest and sowing seasons, keeping up with his younger counterparts.

In 1950, Mohinder Singh, a Kumhar, went to the Philippines under the auspices of his wife's family. Her parents had told him of economic opportunities in a country recovering from the war. So his family and he left for Manila. Being Kumhars, they had little land and fewer prospects for gaining wealth in Jandiali. Thus it was very appealing to emigrate to a place with good potential for riches and people willing to help him get started in a business. He had a lucrative cloth factory in Manila, the proceeds from which he either reinvested or sent back to Punjab to buy land and build a house. Mohinder Singh has retired and resides in Jandiali, while his son and family left for Manila in 1971 to take over Mohinder's profitable businesses.

Jandialian emigration to Britain started around 1950 when the enterprising Zaildar, who was also a bank official in the neighbouring town of Banga, read and heard stories about the vast economic opportunities in England. He resolved to encourage young men to venture abroad and to help them with loans for their passage to England from the village Cooperative Bank.

Jandiali and its environs were crowded with refugees from west Punjab, and many young people agreed with the Zaildar that it made little sense for them to remain and add to the burdens of their family and village when they could make a fortune by going to England. The loan offer was open to all castes and to people from neighbouring communities. The Zaildar was confident that the borrowers would repay their loan when they were able and that they would also invest in the Cooperative Bank. He knew that if a person attempted to escape from his responsibility of repayment, his kinsmen would pressure the errant to honour his commitment. He was correct, and today the Cooperative Bank of Jandiali has lakhs of surplus rupees. Over one million rupees in assets are also visible in the form of *pukka* or brick houses built on the outskirts of the farms around Jandiali, all financed by emigrant capital.

About a dozen men from Jandiali initially availed themselves of this opportunity. None of the pioneer emigrants interviewed had any previous contacts in England. They all left on the faith of what they had heard and with the Zaildar's blessings. Although not the first to leave the village, Bhajan Singh was one of the first to take advantage of the Zaildar's offer. He eventually settled down in industrial Gravesend, a place of numerous job opportunities at that time. Although a Jat, Bhajan Singh came from a relatively poor family. His brother and he had to support their household on the return from their meagre four acres of land which they held in joint ownership with their uncle. They had neither savings nor other assets.

Bhajan Singh's initiative and later assistance to fellow villagers contributed to a large group of Jandialians settling in Gravesend, and his brother helped other Jandialians settle in Leamington Spa. This service raised the izzat of Bhajan Singh and his family from that of a non-entity to one of high respect, outranking many initially wealthier families.

Families pooled all they had to send one of their promising young men with high hopes of success. One such case is of Kavinder Singh who came from a poor Jat family with only seven acres of land to support the families of his father and two uncles (18 people). Hearing about England, they all decided to pool their resources to send Kavinder to England with the hope that upon getting a job he would sponsor them until all family members would be in England, except Kavinder's brother who would stay behind to look after the land. The brother was agreeable, for with seven acres of land and the money from England he could live very well.

Kavinder went to Britain with advice to contact Ravinder Singh, a man from his wife's village, in Bedford. Upon arrival he met Ravinder, who housed and fed Kavinder Singh until he found a job. Kavinder lived frugally, saving money for his father's passage. Upon his father's arrival, both worked to bring Kavinder's uncle. After the males arrived, the female members were sent for, and within two years the whole group was in Bedford living in a common house.

In Sitinder Singh's case, his father felt that it would be to Sitinder's benefit to go to England. Although his father remained behind, his uncles had gone to Leamington Spa. Thus, when Sitinder's father decided that it would be in the best interest of the family for Sitinder to emigrate, his uncle sent him the ticket. He was met at the airport by this uncle, who took him to Leamington Spa and helped him find a job. Sitinder lived with his uncle, worked in a factory, putting in lots of overtime, and saving money. All money was pooled in the household and some was sent to Sitinder's father.

In the meantime, Sitinder's father in Punjab was looking for a nice village girl so that a marriage could be arranged. Being an England-returnee, Sitinder was sought after by the best families with prospective brides. He planned to stay in England about ten years and then return with his wife and family to buy some more land in Punjab.

The Cooperative Bank of Jandiali was only one of many sponsors. Some young men received support from the parents of their intended brides in England; others relied on relatives already settled in Britain; whereas still others sold their belongings and rented their land to finance their passage.[2] When restrictions on passports and exit visas to Britain were imposed by the Indian government in 1955 and 1958, Mohinder Singh, the textile manufacturer in Manila, freely sponsored Jandialians to obtain the proper emigration papers. With exit permits to Manila, these Jandialians arrived in London directly or indirectly. Those who genuinely desired to go always seemed to find the means, although it sometimes meant leaving wives, children, and land in the care of a trustworthy brother or friend.

In 1960, it became apparent that the British government was proposing restrictive legislation for immigration of coloureds. There was a great influx of Punjabis to England to avoid the immigration ban. Wives and children were sent for to join husbands and fathers, followed by extended families. There was great panic to get to England before entry to this wealthy land was closed. People resorted to any means to emigrate. One of of the tactics employed by Jandiali migrants was to familiarize themselves with and use the laws and norms of the host community to their advantage. When in 1962 restrictions were imposed, the Punjabis found ways to circumvent them. One manoeuvre was marriage, because spouses from India could be sponsored. Parliament partially blocked that loophole in 1968 by prohibiting arranged marriages between young men in India with girls in England; however this decision was reversed and spouses, both male and female, were allowed entry.

Whenever a Jandialian is queried about his reasons for emigrating to Britain, the immediate answer is 'for the money', which is definitely a primary or initial motivating factor. Emigration for many was a choice for survival, stemming from economic necessity. The arrival of refugees from West Punjab in 1947 strained agricultural resources. Alternative means of livelihood were limited. If a Jat is unable to farm, he prefers military service for the prestige it carries. Punjabis in rural India generally refuse factory work because of its subservient nature. However, this is not the case in England, where Jats will take up any job and work overtime to amass wealth.

Information, often inaccurate, about conditions in England came during hard times, enticing many to emigrate. Whether successful or destitute, the English returnee always glorified his position in Britain, and the wealth sent back or displayed by visiting emigrants gave credibility to their claims. The following letter, written by an émigré to his brother, illustrates the exaggerated information villagers received concerning England.

My job in Gravesend is very easy. I go to work at 8 a.m. and push the green button to make the machine go. I sit in my chair until mid-morning, when I push the red button to stop the machine and take a half-hour tea break. After tea, I return and push the green button to make the machine go and sit in my chair until lunch. At lunchtime I push the red button to stop the machine, take an hour off until 1 p.m. when I return. I push the green button again to make the machine go. At tea-time in the afternoon, the red button is pushed to stop the machine and we take a half-hour off for tea, and then again I push the green button to start the machine until it is time to go home at 5 p.m. Then, I push the red button and stop the machine. For this I make Rs 1800 a month.

To a villager averaging Rs 200 a month—that is, if he was lucky and had a successful harvest, England sounded like paradise. The author of this letter had figured his wages on the black market rate of Rs 30 to the pound as compared to the legal exchange of Rs 18. When the recipient finally arrived in England, he found his brother sweating in a cement factory, his hands calloused and bruised, not at the soft job he had boasted about. The émigré brother claimed that he had lost the easy job and had to work in a cement factory.

To entice customers, travel agents also related gloriously exaggerated stories about England as the land of opportunity, with numerous highly paid jobs and ample wealth for all. They did not worry about the client's financial position and extended easy credit. The emigrant was not aware that upon his arrival in England the representatives of the agents would extract every pound he earned until the debt was paid off.

Black marketeers and illegal immigration racketeers lured unsuspecting villagers to rely totally on them to take care of everything. Some trusting villagers, who generally disliked dealings with bureaucrats and government officials, accepted the word of agents without realizing that they were being smuggled into England.

Roshan Singh's experience illustrates the problems he encountered in 1969. Roshan's father went to Phagwara to sell grain and happened to talk to a travel agent. Having heard from fellow villagers about the opportunities in England, the agent's tales seemed reasonable. Thus he arranged for Roshan to go to England, reasoning that Roshan would return to Punjab in a few years with wealth that far exceeded their dreams. Although his father did not realize it, Roshan was to be smuggled into England. It was only after arriving that Roshan suspected something was wrong, but it was too late.

He soon got a job and started paying his debt. However, he was informed that he would have to pay much more to keep his sponsors from telling the British authorities about his illegal entry. Roshan saw that he could not afford to make the necessary payments, so he joined a political party to which he pledged loyalty in return for protection. Thus, though he may have wanted to maintain an independent stance, he could no longer do so now.

To give an instance of another form of exploitation: Chand Kaur wanted to help her son come to England in 1968, and an agent said that he would arrange everything for £800; but when Chand Kaur paid the money in cash she did not receive a receipt. She never heard from the agent or her son. She could not go to the police for fear they would prosecute her and not punish the agent, especially since she had no proof. She had learned in Punjab that the police were people one does not trust, and as far as she knew, the English police were no different. All she could do was mourn her missing son.

In England, agents sometimes persuaded parents to send for their sons or relatives, promising to take care of all the necessary details. After the money had been paid, the relative did not arrive, and the agent was never heard of again. The defrauded immigrant in England had no recourse to justice, for he did not want to expose himself or his fellowmen to the police. Besides, since Punjabis paid cash, they had no proof to support their claims. Those relatives who were successfully, but illegally, smuggled in were blackmailed by agents with the threat of exposure and deportation. Punjabis had to stick together for mutual protection against such unscrupulous exploiters. Thus, political groups such as the Indian Workers' Association were essential for the Punjabi immigrant's protection in England.

Besides escaping poverty, many migrated to avoid shame. Exaggerated reports of actions being hidden in England enticed those who faced degradation due to a daughter or sister running off with another man, an unfaithful wife, or a perfidious mother. Honour-conscious Punjabis emigrated to England and other places with hopes of redeeming that lost izzat caused by an errant member of the family. Many fled from their wives, hoping to hide in Britain.[3] But given the close Punjabi social network and efficient communication, the village spouse eventually arrived on her husband's doorstep with her children, much to the chagrin of her husband and often his white woman. Generally, a man of honour had to fulfil his obligations to his family once he was discovered. Escape seemed virtually impossible for any Punjabi in spite of stories of being lost in the crowd. Baldev Singh's is a case in point. He left Punjab for England in 1952, leaving his wife and two daughters, vowing that he would return shortly. In England he met an Irish girl, fell in love, and married her without telling her about his family in India. He had a good job and was living well when one day there was a knock on his front door, and he stood face-to-face with his Indian wife and daughters. Financial help from her brothers and information from village-mates had enabled her to find her spouse. Baldev now supports both families, who live in separate English towns. Family honour and fear of his Punjabi wife's brothers has forced him to provide for her as well as his English family.

Though many Punjabi emigrants left India because they were poor, there were situations like that of Meer Singh where even rich young men desired to leave. Meer Singh, who quit medical school to migrate to Canada, came from a rich zamindar family. Not only did his father control 1,500 acres of land in Punjab, Uttar Pradesh, and Rajasthan, but money was plentiful. The older son immigrated to Yuba City, California, because he could not get along with his stepmother. On a visit home to Jandiali, Jeet Singh was asked by his family to help his young stepbrother emigrate. Jeet replied that he did not think young Meer Singh had the ability to do well abroad. This was a challenge to Meer Singh. He decided to give up his future medical career and his father's riches to accept the proposed marriage to a Punjabi girl in Canada. When he arrived in Canada, he found that he did not even like the girl's looks. However, he married her to stay in Canada and save his father's izzat. This young man, who has been working as a factory labourer in Canada, could have lived in great affluence had he stayed in Punjab.

Mahesh Lal was another example, for he was a Chamar whose father had amassed considerable wealth. As a result, he sent Mahesh Lal (B.A. degree from Punjab University) to England. Despite his education, Mahesh was only able to get a job as a factory labourer. However, he helped the illiterate Jats in Gravesend with income-tax forms and other items necessary for getting along in England. Although Mahesh did not make much money, he bought a house, the down payment for which came from his father in India.

Although the family was well off, Mahesh Lal's father saw a chance for social mobility for his son in England—a rich Chamar in India was still a Chamar. In England those of a low caste did not carry the stigma they had in India, even in the immigrant community. Mahesh was better off in England than he would have been in India. The Punjabi Jats in Gravesend continued to view Mahesh as a Chamar despite his education and economic status, but he achieved a position of leadership in the community.

Some Punjabis ventured abroad as a security investment for well-to-do-relatives. The rich knew that with land ceiling legislation in Punjab in the offing acreage and wealth were vulnerable to government control or confiscation. Sons and

daughters were sent or married abroad to ensure the family
members a place and position. It was not uncommon, however,
for several siblings to be living in different countries—England,
Canada, or the United States. Decisions as to who emigrated
and where were based on abilities and opportunities in the
potential host countries. If the conditions in one country became
politically objectionable or economically difficult, kinsmen in
another country helped sponsor their relatives' entry into their
own adopted country. If an area was viewed as financially lucrative, village and family members pooled their resources to finance migration to that particular area. These tactics are well
illustrated in the case of Trilochan Singh and Resham Singh.

Trilochan went to Hong Kong and, with the help of friends
there, bought a small hotel. Upon gaining financial stability, he
brought his wife and three sons to Hong Kong and taught his
sons the hotel business. Fearing disturbances in Hong Kong's
economy and the threat of a possible Communist takeover,
Trilochan Singh sent one son to New York, another to Toronto,
and the third to London. With their father providing the initial
capital needed, all three started hotel businesses in their respective cities. Trilochan Singh frequently remarks: 'If things go
wrong in Hong Kong or any of the other cities, we can all get
help from the son who is in the most prosperous area.'

Resham Singh was a rich landowner in Punjab; he had over
100 acres of land. He feared that land ceiling legislation was
about to be enacted, so he sent his younger son to California to
earn money and buy farm land. The bright young boy not only
bought land there, but traded some of his father's land with
Californian Punjabis who wanted to return to Punjab. Seven
acres of California land for one acre in Punjab. Upon arrival in
California, the son had learned of elderly California Jats who
were homesick and longed to return to Punjab. He made deals
with them and is a prosperous farmer outside Stockton. As
Resham Singh often states: 'If my land in Punjab is confiscated
by the government, I shall go abroad to my son.' Also, he has
already transferred a great deal of his money abroad into his
son's account.

Some Punjabis forsook education for high wages and menial
jobs. Bir Singh is a good example of such a case. After receiving
his Master's degree in engineering, he decided to go to the
United States for higher education. Having been accepted at

San Diego State College, he travelled via Britain. A friend in England convinced him of the enormous wealth he could gain by working in a British factory as opposed to being a poor graduate student in the United States. He gave up his plans for a higher education and stayed on in England. He got a job in heavy industry, and in 1970 he was still working at the same factory and putting in many hours of overtime to add money to his savings account. Bir Singh was only one of many Punjabis who left to pursue higher education but decided to seek financial gain through factory jobs. It was not uncommon for them to drop out of school to take blue-collar jobs, especially when enticed by gains through overtime and double pay. Tangible signs of prosperity were not easy to resist.

Impediments to emigration affected the Hindus more than the Sikh Jats. The former were more concerned about maintaining purity than the latter, whose major worry was not purity but the character of those living abroad and how it affected family izzat. The Sikh Jats feared that an emigrant would start smoking, drinking excessively, become lazy for lack of physical farm work, or, worst of all, marry an English girl. How these factors influenced thinking are portrayed by Harjan Singh who wanted to go to England to gain the prestige he saw in England-returnees who showed off their nylon pajamas and used English words. His father would not let him go. Harjan's father had been in England for five years and was aware of the pitfalls. He feared his son would start drinking excessively, associate with English girls, and not be able to cope with the hard factory work. Besides, Harjan was an only son; if he left there would be no one to look after the parents and light their funeral pyre. The elders did not want to lose their old-age security. They feared that Harjan would forget about his family and become hypnotized by the glitter of English life. Harjan was forced to stay in Punjab. Beyond being corrupted by English ways, it was more important to live up to one's family obligations, especially for the sons.

It was the mother who exerted a special influence on an erring son by sending him guilt-inducing letters claiming that she was dying of a broken heart due to his neglect. Some elderly women went further and resorted to hunger strikes until they heard that the offspring had improved his erring ways and/or of his plans to return. Few young men were so callous as to be able to live with such guilt and the added condemnation of the Punjabi Sikh Jat community. In some circumstances, the wife was left behind in Jandiali to look after and ensure the well-being of her ageing parents-in-law. The husband continued to work in England, sent money home for the support of the family, and occasionally paid a visit.

While it was sometimes difficult for young men to receive family and community sanction to emigrate, the restrictions for girls were far greater. No respectable Jandiali family allowed a daughter to emigrate abroad alone. She could go if a marriage had been finalized in England, and then, too, it was imperative for her to be properly chaperoned until her wedding day, when she became the responsibility of her in-laws. It was contended in Jandiali that once a young girl went to England she would become spoiled. There was particular concern among Punjabis that British education and western exposure afforded girls too much independence, making them bad spouses. Therefore, it was no surprise that an immigrant parent preferred a girl from the village, even with minimal dowry (£200 or just passage from India), to a Punjabi Sikh Jat immigrant girl raised in England with a larger dowry (as high as £4,000) and a reputation above reproach.

At least three men from Jandiali did not allow their wives or daughters to accompany them to England for fear that English life would have an adverse effect on them. Ujjal Singh lived in England for five years, worked hard and made good money, while his wife and family stayed behind in Jandiali. He returned to Jandiali and lived well, boasting about his good fortune and life-style. However, he was more liberal than his brother and allowed his two younger daughters to cycle to Phagwara with other girls to pursue their studies, at least until they finished their schooling.

A person's sex and position in the family hierarchy were factors considered in making a decision about emigration, although age was not necessarily a constraint. Men and women in their seventies and eighties emigrated, sometimes lying about their age just to be with their family. Some elderly Jandialians who held positions of prestige and esteem in the village stayed home, not because they were too old, but because they feared that they would lack respect in England. Besides, they would not have the social support of their fellow villagers with whom they had grown, suffered, and rejoiced throughout their lives. Villagers viewed themselves as a team, and with age, money and material goods became less important than respect and honour, the latter being viewed as a reward for a lifetime of work. The success of a family was measured in the village mainly by the evaluation of village-mates. Although more research needs to be done in this realm, as a general rule, the elderly from prestigious families are not as likely to emigrate as the elders of relatively low izzat families.

As has been noted, the Jat's greatest concern was for his land. Sohan Singh, a Jandialian, remained in the village to maintain the family land while his father and two brothers went to England. Kartar Singh and his sons functioned on the basis of a two-year stint in England and one year in Jandiali, farming the family land. Few Jats, if any, left Jandiali without ensuring that their land was adequately taken care of and managed. If an emigrant's land-holdings were in peril, he returned immediately to amend the situation. Kartar Singh, mentioned above, and his sons migrated to Gravesend in the early 1960s, leaving his land in the care of a cousin. When Kartar Singh heard that his cousin was claiming squatter's rights, he immediately returned from England, leaving behind a well-paid job and his wife. His sons and their families stayed in England with the understanding that they (the two sons and he) would move annually between Gravesend and Jandiali. This was an inconvenience and a financial loss, but keeping the village land within the immediate family was most important. They did, however, build themselves a modern-style house for comfortable living.

For Punjabis in general and Jandialians in particular, emigration was a traditional means of coping with the harsh circumstances that life offered. This tactic has been resorted to by Europeans for hundreds of years. Poverty was only one of many motivating factors that encouraged emigration. The exaggerated portrayal of conditions abroad, enhancing one's izzat and gaining a better education, were some of the other factors to be considered while deciding whether one should or should not go abroad. And, as this study will further show, the emigrants are always in a dilemma and never really sure if their decision was the right one.

CHAPTER IV

THE BIRTH OF GRAVESINDIA[1]
(1947-1959)

Gravesend

The host community, Gravesend, on which this study focuses, lies about twenty miles east of London on the River Thames, across from Tilbury harbour (Figure 3). Being a part of the Greater London industrial region, Gravesend naturally became a likely focus for the post-War immigration of Punjabis. Its western sector is crowded with paper mills, cable, rubber, printing, cement, and engineering works; shipbuilding, ship repair yards, and ancillary industries boost Gravesend's economy and make it an ideal community for immigrant labour.

In 1971 roughly 5,600, or 10 per cent of Gravesend's population of 55,160, was made up of immigrants. There were about 120 Pakistanis, 20 West Indians, a few families from Malta, and the remainder of Indian origin. Of the latter, most were Punjabi Sikh Jats, mainly from villages in Doaba;[2] about 20 per cent were Ramgardiahs (a number of whom were Kenyan Asians), a few were low caste, and 1 per cent were Hindus.

In Gravesend the Sikh Jats prefer heavy labour jobs in foundries and factories. Despite the hard work and irregular hours, construction is considered the most lucrative profession. Comparatively few Indians hold white-collar jobs, although there are four bank clerks, one postal official, sixteen school teachers,[3] two accountants, and one Kenyan Asian female secretary in the borough planning department. There are sixteen South Asian doctors and twenty-three nurses, mainly from non-Jat backgrounds, in Gravesend's National Health Service. Some enterprising Punjabis have branched into grocery, clothing, and insurance businesses, whereas many others have jobs outside Gravesend and commute daily as far as London. There

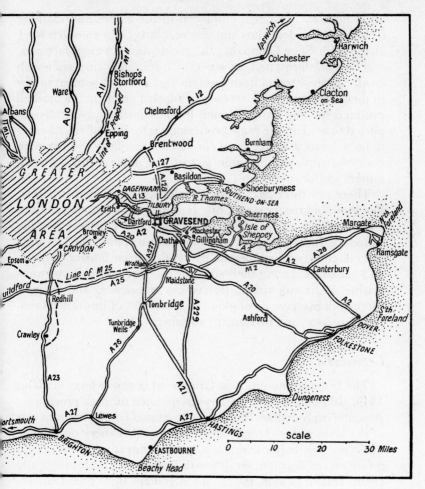

Figure 3. Location of Gravesend

are a number of women employed in the zipper and clothing factories of London who commute regularly; other women work at the Bata Shoe Company, the pickle and Kleenex factories, and on truck farms picking vegetables. Indian businessmen with small concerns travel from London and contract women to sew in their own homes. They come regularly to pick up the finished products for marketing. Young Punjabi girls are generally expected to work in the same professions as their mothers, whether it be a factory, store, farm, or home. Similarly, young men prefer to work in the same factories as their fathers, grandfathers and/or uncles.

There are three Sikh pubs (two of which opened in 1971), five Punjabi grocery stores, one Indian sweet shop, two drapers (stores which sell ready-made clothes and fabrics especially suited for Indian outfits), and one Indian restaurant.[4] At least three factory workers peddle everything from fabrics to china and glassware during their spare or off-duty hours. Two enterprising Sikhs run driver instruction businesses, and at least three Indians have a conglomerate business of insurance sales, travel agency, and investment advising.

Gravesindia

The Indian community in Gravesend began to form in about 1949, although Asians may have frequented the area previously. A young Sikh pedlar, Bhuta Singh, gained employment in one of the local paper companies. When an oil refinery on the Isle of Grain was being constructed, the innovative Bhuta Singh set up an employment service with British contractors to supply cheap Indian labour. He recruited Indians from East London, Birmingham, and other areas, brought them to Gravesend, and, for a fee, provided them with jobs, handled all their paperwork (including social security, income-tax, and health forms), and rented them rooms in his house. While his wife remained in India, Bhuta Singh lived with an English woman who, because she worked at the social security office, knew how to handle these details. Generally, Bhuta Singh guaranteed a set wage to these non-English-speaking Punjabis, pocketing anything extra from their pay packet. Bhuta Singh not only received a commission from the contractors, but prospered from the rent and fees. He held this monopoly for several years until other immigrants sufficiently mastered the English language to handle their own affairs. The lack of knowledge of English and the legal system made many of the early Punjabi Sikh Jat immigrants insecure. They had to face many hardships, as the following narrative indicates:

I came to England in 1949, straight from the village of Paragpur, near Jullundur. My father sent me abroad to study biology and chemistry at an English university. A friend in East London persuaded me to make money rather than study. As I was not successful job-hunting in the London area, I went with some friends to Gravesend. This was a few months after Bhuta Singh came. Being coloured and foreign, we had difficulty finding a place to live in, for no Englishman wanted us in his home. Finally, some Irishman helped us acquire a room with Miss Smith on Queens Street, near what is now Thandi's Sikh pub. All six of us lived in a room which had one double bed and two singles. Since we were on shift-work, we alternated using the beds. We earned £4–10s a week and paid £2–10s per head for the room and a light lunch.

After a few weeks, three of us found cheaper and better lodging with an old lady on The Grove. We only paid £1–5s a week for bed and a breakfast consisting of stale sausages and eggs. One Saturday we complained to her about the food and went out to play hockey. While we were out, she had her son place our friend (who was asleep as he had been on the night shift) and all our belongings on the street. Upon returning late, we apologized profusely and begged her to take us back. She swore at us and shut the door in our bewildered faces. We finally went back to Miss Smith, who absolutely refused to let us in. It was almost dark and we had nowhere to go. After more pleading, Miss Smith gave in with the promise from us that we would never complain or leave. We had learned our lesson.

For most of my colleagues who knew only a little English at the time, finding a job was a difficult task. I was finally successful at Bowaters,[5] because I knew a little English. Whenever the interviewer asked me a question, I answered, 'Yes, Sir' or 'No, Sir', depending on what I guessed the answer should be. I was hired and told to report at 2 p.m., and I obliged. Later I learned that my interviewer was hard of hearing!

Our bosses soon realized that we Punjabis were hard working and they were pleased with us. Therefore, whenever we brought in a friend and asked for a job, the boss was agreeable. We always scanned the newspapers, looking for jobs for unemployed friends and relatives in Gravesend, elsewhere in England, or still in Punjab.

To learn English, we bought newspapers and practised reading to each other. Nowadays, our wives learn English from the telly, which we did not have access to.

In the early days, there wasn't much discrimination. We were served in the pubs, but only in the Public Bar, as we were prohibited from entering the Saloon Bar. The English, however, did not like us going out with their women. One instance in particular was when we met some English girls and took them to a local dance. When the girls went to the make-up room, we were kicked out. Several days later when we saw the ladies, they inquired as to what had happened, and we had to explain. If we stopped and talked to white girls, Englishmen made snide and threatening comments.

The early residents of Gravesindia were almost all men because it was cheaper to leave the family in Punjab, where the cost of living was lower; besides, a single man had the mobility to shift to better employment if necessary. When enough money was amassed,[6] the goal was to return to Punjab to begin a life of ease, becoming a *Bara Sahib*—an important man in the eyes of village-mates. During these early years emigration was selective, and only those men ventured forth to England who either had little in their home village, or were bright sons whose families considered them most likely to succeed. No kin group wasted their assets on a member who was incapable of yielding a high return. Thus, the early emigrants from Jandiali were competent, responsible, and innovative men who wanted to make as much money as fast as they possibly could.

These early emigrants lived in rooming houses, owned primarily for renting cheaply to migrant workers. Life in these men's houses was austere and unhygienic, but was the cheapest accommodation available. Harbachan Singh describes it in the following way:

Conditions in our men's house in those early years were deplorable. Our house had only one kitchen, a bath, and one outdoor toilet to serve forty of us residing there. Two of us on different shifts teamed up to share a single bed in a bedroom that was so overcrowded with cots that the floor was not visible.

We preferred Indian food to the bland English diet, and each man was responsible for his own meals. As shifts were generally staggered, things did not get too crowded in the kitchen; but the cooker was continually operating. We soon discovered that if we bought *atta* (flour) and *dal* (lentils) in large quantities, we could save a lot of money. So we would join in and get 100-pound sacks of atta and large amounts of dal—thus saving considerably on our food bill.

Some men in the early years even lived in barns or animal stalls, so those of us in a house considered ourselves lucky. Of course, it was crowded, but we helped each other and got along. Our main aim was to work hard, live frugally, and make money. I wanted to go home with honour, so I was willing to put up with this inconvenience— especially when I realized that every pound saved equalled thirty-six rupees.[7] Besides, the house was just a place to sleep in, nothing else— our social life revolved around meeting people either at work or in the pub.

These deplorable conditions motivated Bhajan Singh of Jandiali and his associates to buy a house to help fellow Punjabis. Their house became so famous that every non-English-speaking Indian arriving at the Gravesend train station was automatically taken to Bhajan Singh's place on Wakefield Street. Although immigrants later moved to other locations, they continued to use the Wakefield Street address; this aroused the suspicions of the Health Department, which sent an inspector to check on the one thousand or so immigrants who had given that address when registering for the National Health Service.

In the early years, some cultural values were compromised as the Jats attempted to adapt to English life and improve their financial positions. When the number of immigrants was still low, Jats, Chamars, and Ramgardiahs often lived in the same boarding house regardless of caste barriers. This situation changed only with the influx of women and children. However, there was no apparent caste distinction in places of employment although it is impossible to gauge the inner feelings regarding caste biases. Higher castes did not complain openly about sweeping, picking up cigarette butts, or doing anything which would bring a good wage, even though they would never consider doing such things in Punjab. For example, Harbachan Singh, upon arriving in Gravesend, got a job as a janitor at Bowaters. 'It was repulsive', he stated, 'cleaning showers and lavatories, and picking up cigarette butts off the floor.' To Harbachan, however, being a janitor and doing polluting work was better than being shamed by not sending earnings back to his family in Punjab. Besides, they would never know how he earned the money; they only knew what he told them, and he never mentioned being a janitor.[8] Harbachan Singh had no choice. He had to show the home village that he was successful, even if this meant compromising caste dictates. Maintaining his purity and being a failure in the eyes of his village-mates was far more degrading than being a janitor. And, if word did get back to Jandiali, he could always deny it, saying that the informer was jealous.

The following situation will explain that kin loyalty was also of extreme importance to the émigré. Meet Singh and his brothers exemplify the value of family to early migrants.

Meet Singh and his brothers were a cohesive unit in Gravesend. Meet Singh, the eldest of the three, had come first and then brought his two younger brothers soon thereafter. Because of his exceptionally hard work, Meet Singh was able to get his brothers jobs in the foundry where he worked. They put in a lot of overtime and made good money. Soon they brought their wives and children, and initially they all lived together in a jointly-owned house. The brothers were a force to be reckoned with in Gravesend. Help one brother, all were grateful; harm one, be ready to answer to all of them and their friends. If, after a drinking spree, one of the brothers became involved in a fight, his adversary had to face all three sooner or later, no matter what the issue or who was at fault. Likewise, if one of the brothers learned of better employment, he took the position and the other two followed suit.

As helpful as they were to each other, they were not unaware of other relatives and village-mates, and frequently helped them with loans and jobs. For this their izzat in Gravesend and also in their home village was greatly enhanced. When Meet Singh returned to Punjab on a holiday, his village treated him well. What was originally a humble family became a highly respected one. When Meet Singh wrote to the village panchayat, it now considered his wishes seriously.

Primary loyalty was to kinsmen. Brothers helped brothers obtain jobs, preferring to work together. When a Punjabi immigrant needed a job, every kinsman in England helped him find one, especially if the kin and/or village ties were close. Amiable relations in Punjab were continued in England. People who were close in Punjab desired to work and live together. As the Punjabis often remarked, 'loyalty to one's own salt was unquestioned and unconditional'. Male social networks were tight, and news about employment opportunities spread fast. A man who learned about a job first called his brothers, then village-mates, and finally friends. When a new Punjabi arrived, each spoke to his foreman to find out if the newcomer could be hired. Since the Punjabis were strong and hard working, and accepted jobs the English thought undignified, employers liked to hire them.

The Punjabis in England, and Gravesend in particular, saw opportunities as a means to help friends. In their estimation, there was enough in England for everyone. It was the goal of these Jats prospering in England to help the less fortunate, because aiding others was *seva* and gave one a high evaluation *robh* among other immigrants and possibly a basis for future political power. Sponsoring someone to England was an investment which would be repaid by the grateful receiver to uphold his family honour. The recipient would also become a permanent and loyal supporter of the donor, establishing a relationship of general reciprocity.

Since the Gravesindian community during this time comprised mostly males with only two nuclear families, men did not generally write to Punjab informing people in the village of deviant behaviour. Males in England lived as they pleased. Generally, infidelity to wife or family in India was overlooked by fellow Jats in Gravesend, unless a brother-in-law was unfaithful to one's sister. Breaking norms was acceptable as long as an individual did not exploit his own people. Undoubtedly, the behaviour and fidelity of a man was only of prime concern to his spouse in Punjab, where rumours and gossip about erring husbands abounded. However, as long as the man helped kinsmen and village-mates, and continued to provide for his family in Jandiali, he was accepted by the villagers and allowed the high position of an England-returnee. Rumours and gossip about unacceptable behaviour in England were not given much credence during this early period and were often excused as coming from a jealous tale-teller. Gravesend–Jandiali communications were not sufficiently established to exert control from the place of origin. Besides, the number of women and children was not high enough to influence male conformity.

Separateness from the host community did not warrant British evaluations of their behaviour. Thus, outside the arena of employment, few restrictions were imposed on the Gravesindians as long as they did not impinge on the host community or harm fellow Punjabis.

Initially, both political power and leadership were in the hands of cultural brokers like Bhuta Singh and paternalistic fellowmen like Bhajan Singh who were able to transcend the barrier between the English and Punjabis. Their knowledge of English ways and familiarity with bureaucratic forms made their services essential to new arrivals. Most immigrants tolerated being cheated and exploited by agents as long as they continued making more money than before. Escaping the stranglehold of these intermediaries was virtually impossible as long as the Gravesindian spoke no English. The broker's total control over his naïve clients is apparent from the following testimony:

I came to Bedford with the help of my brother, but I was unable to find a job. Some friends told me about Gravesend, so I ventured there. Upon arrival I saw Bhuta Singh and immediately got a job on the Isle of Grain. He arranged everything for me, gave me a room in one of his houses on Cutmore Street, took care of my papers, and I was at work the next day.

While on the job, he was our translator and interpreter for the English foreman. He was not really needed because we could usually communicate enough with the Englishman and knew what to do. When pay day came, Bhuta Singh waited next to the pay master and took each pay packet from the cashier, withdrew his portion, and gave us what was left. I still do not know what my proper or exact wage was at that time.

During the early years, the Gravesindians opted for the job that paid the best. However, he might work at a factory for lower wages per hour if he had overtime options. The goal was to earn as much as possible; even if working twice as long meant earning only one-and-a-half times more, the job with longer hours was taken. The total wage earned was important, not the wage per hour. Jugga Singh, for example, upon arrival in Gravesend, worked for the Imperial Paper Company. He took the job because at that time it had the promise of overtime which a clerical job did not have. 'I needed the money', he said.

Even though the wages at Imperial were lower per hour, I could work overtime. We would rest and then work several shifts continuously. The pay was time and a half for the first overtime shift, and double time for the second consecutive overtime shift, enabling me to work for a couple of days straight without a break.[9] This was done on weekends, since the English did not like to work on weekends, which made no difference to us.

After six months, my brother-in-law told me about a factory job in Bedford where the pay was better and overtime work was also possible. So I moved to Bedford immediately, lived with my brother-in-law, and worked there. Not having my family here, I could move easily.

Although a man preferred to be with his own group, this did not prohibit him from moving on to better opportunities. Such a move might even cause social and emotional problems because of lack of support from one's kinsmen; however, at that time priority was given to gaining wealth, and most of them worked unbelievably hard. But working extra hard and long hours was not always by choice, as is evident from Piara Singh's situation. He was employed at a nearby automobile factory where he was the only immigrant in a speedometer assembly division. Like his English counterparts, he put together 75 units a day. After being on the job several months, his foreman instructed him to assemble 90 units per day. He talked to his fellow British workers and, following their advice, told his superior that he would try to oblige, but maintained the previous speed. Not seeing an improvement, the foreman moved Piara Singh to a slot on the assembly line where the work was more difficult and taxing.

After several weeks in the more difficult position, Piara Singh was returned to the speedometer assembly unit and informed that if he did not turn out 90 units a day he would be fired. He complied, and although he tried to explain his predicament to his fellow white workers, they did not understand and resented him. However, the tale does not end here, for after a month the foreman again returned and told Piara to assemble 105 units a day. When Piara's production did not increase, he was again put on the assembly line, returned after a time, and threatened with the loss of his job if he did not obey. He worked harder to comply and keep his well-paid job.

The immigrant worker neither had the support of unions nor the knowledge of English ways to deal with such pressures exerted by managements. Employers coerced Asians to work much harder than their English counterparts. The Indian's position was a difficult one. He did not want to lose his job; yet, if he performed according to instructions he aroused the resentment of his English colleagues and periodically became the target of their frustrations—they could not or would not understand the vulnerable position that he was in. Employers liked to hire Indians because of their obedience; and, if one performed well, others were liable to fill vacancies. Therefore, in the factory where Piara Singh worked, the speedometer assembly division eventually became an entirely Punjabi area, much to the resentment of the English, who complained that Indians were taking over their jobs. It is interesting that the antagonism was directed at the Punjabis and not the managers.

The early life of Gravesindia revolved around men's houses, jobs, pubs, and eventually the local gurdwara. As Banta Singh states,

I worked hard overtime and took all the available weekend jobs. Usually our life was quite regular and simple. It was on the job and during the bus ride that we visited and shared local and home news. After work we showered and cleaned up before frequenting the pub to quench our thirst with a good beer. We always went to the public bar because it was cheaper. We had a good time for an hour or so before returning to our boarding house. After Bhajan Singh brought over the Granth Sahib, we had weekly services in his home, where a room was set aside for our Holy Book. We could go there any time, but it was during the weekly service that the whole community came together.

Since hot water was plentiful at the factory, the émigré showered before returning; the bath in the men's house was not in great demand, affording the landlord considerable saving on utilities. Practically every Jat emulated the British custom of frequenting their local pub to socialize and enjoy draught beer. The 'local' became, and still is today, a primary social centre for the Gravesindians. When Bhajan Singh brought the Granth Sahib from Punjab, its location became another place for congregating.

Starting a gurdwara was, and still is, a high priority in a new

Sikh community, so in 1953 Bhajan Singh sent for a Guru Granth Sahib and set aside one room in his house for Sikh worship.[10] The Gravesindians proudly claim that they hosted the first *akhand path* in England. In 1957, despite protests from the local English population, a house was bought at 55 Edwin Street to serve as a gurdwara. Within a year, however, this house became too small for the services and meetings.[11] So, they invested in an old church building which is the gurdwara today.

As in other areas with a purely male population, girls were often picked up at pubs. In Gravesend they were taken to 10 Wakefield Street, where rooms were rented for 10 shillings a night, without breakfast. It was later revealed that Pakistani[12] girls came from London on a weekly basis for business.

It is difficult to gauge the attitude of the English of Gravesend during the early years. Since Jandialians and other Punjabis were in Gravesend for the purpose of earning money, discrimination did not concern the immigrants as long as they continued to obtain suitable employment. The local newspaper did not reveal any animosity toward the Gravesindians during the fifties, although they were restricted to the public bar and discouraged from dating local girls. The children of the two first Punjabi families in Gravesend claim that they felt genuinely welcome, were willingly helped by their teachers in school, and were accepted by their white playmates. The racism which had emerged in areas such as Nottinghill and Smethwick was virtually non-existent in Gravesend, where tolerance and a certain degree of amicability continued to prevail.

During this time, hardworking Punjabis were in great demand with local English contractors and factories to meet the labour shortages still resulting from the War. The English community valued Punjabi workmen, and since they were relatively few in number and laboured on jobs the English did not want, they satisfied a vital need of the community-at-large.

How people perceive their situation and relationship to other groups affects their behaviour (Merton 1968:269–334 and Lynch 1968 and 1969). Based on village life, the Jats in England perceived themselves to be superior and stronger than others. This opinion was not shared by other South Asians, who, along with college-educated and urbanized Indians in Gravesend,

blamed the uneducated Jat villagers for the low opinion the
English had of Indians. These new rural arrivals were considered vulgar and shabbily dressed by the sophisticated urban
Indians, who criticized the Jats for wearing indigenous styles,
using cutlery improperly, drinking excessively, and smelling of
curry. This, however, was seldom said openly, and even if it
was, the Jandialian émigré would have paid little attention to
it because he was secure in his Jat superiority and proud of it.
If anything, an Englishman's comment carried far greater
weight than that of a fellow Indian, even if the latter had more
experience and a superior education.

The Gravesindian also emulated some British behaviour. In
the early days, the prestige of British culture was such that the
first two Gravesindian families raised their children in the
English fashion. The parents continued to maintain Punjabi
dress, eating habits, and culture while encouraging their
children to associate with their English playmates and dress in
English-style clothes. These Anglicized families were neither
chided nor condemned by other Punjabis in Gravesend who,
at that time, were predominantly male.

The vast majority of Gravesend Sikhs shaved their beards and
cut their hair to get jobs in England. They were made to realize
the danger of long hair and it was thought that beards became
entangled in heavy machinery. Though perhaps necessary for
adaptation, this was a serious compromise of their beliefs even
if not an attempt to imitate the British. By far and large, however, they remained proud of their Sikh identity, effecting only
those compromises that were really necessary.

Jandiali and her emigrants

At the same time in their home village of Jandiali, the emigrants and their families commanded more power and authority
than they had had prior to emigration. The stories of Bhajan
Singh and Sajan Singh appropriately illustrate this point. By
helping their fellow Punjabis emigrate and by providing moral
and financial help, they were able to fulfil their respective
religious and cultural dictates of *seva*, thus gaining *robh* and
izzat for themselves and their extended families.

The relatively few Jandiali emigrants of this early period

became quite influential on their visits home. Every action of theirs was impressive and automatically correlated with foreign wealth. The émigré encouraged this image by walking around the village, showing off his made-in-England clothes and injecting a few English words into his conversation. He also brought lavish presents for his kin and friends from England and demonstrated his wealth by paying for refreshments or buying things for those with whom he associated. Every village boy hero-worshipped the returnee and dreamed of the day he would go across the seas. Thus, boys in the village sought to learn English so that they would have no difficulty conversing when they migrated. Education in subjects such as mathematics and engineering was popular because of the prospects they offered. In general, only those English traits which were considered superior by the Punjabis were adopted.

In these early years, a band of rural Punjabi Jats settled in Gravesend and helped others come abroad. Their purpose was to save as much capital as possible; therefore, they lived in an austere manner. They used their situation to amass wealth and exert authority in their community of origin. They had to rely on each other, and those who had no kinsmen or village-mates to help them were at somewhat of a disadvantage. Generally, there was a freedom from the social strictures of their sending community; thus home impressions of emigrants to England were manipulated to perpetuate the myth of Jat esteem in Britain. Also social distance was maintained between them and the host community. But this simple pattern of a temporary abode for them in Gravesend was to change dramatically with the coming of the 1960s.

CHAPTER V

BEATING THE BAN ON
IMMIGRATION
(1960-1962)

The consequences of the sudden influx

The threat and later implementation of the 1962 immigration restrictions changed the situation for the Gravesend–Jandiali migrants. They were faced with the possibility of friends and relatives being prohibited from entering England. What new strategy would be employed? Would the Punjabis unite and become belligerent? What would the ramifications be? For the Gravesend–Jandiali migrant, new adaptive behaviour had to be implemented to overcome these obstacles.

The Gravesindians shared the response of other Punjabis in England to the proposed restrictions on immigration to Britain, i.e. to persuade relatives, friends, and village-mates to rush to Britain before new laws were imposed. Those in Gravesend were willing to help with fares, aid in finding jobs, and assist in settlement. As one Sikh wrote:

Those who desire to come to England must do so immediately; if they don't like it, they can always return to Punjab. At least they will have had the opportunity to consider Britain as an alternative to village life; you must avail of the chance before the doors to this land of opportunity are permanently closed.

True to this thinking, wives, children, relatives, village-mates, and friends arrived at Heathrow, inaugurating the population explosion of Punjabis in the United Kingdom. Where previously there had been pockets of Jats, there were now full-fledged communities within, but separate from, the host society.

The following illustrations portray the response of these immigrants to the impending restrictions. Deep Singh was living in a men's house when he perceived that if he waited, his family

might never be able to come to England. Immediately he sent
tickets to his wife and children and rented a flat from his friend,
Resham Singh. After a few months, however, their two wives
argued concerning the children, so Deep Singh borrowed
money from a friend and bought a house near a village-mate
on The Avenue. It was close to town, so his wife could walk to
the grocery store. It was near friends, so she could socialize.
Transportation to his work was accessible, so they were quite
comfortable.

Similarly, when immigration restrictions were perceived,
Arjan Singh and his wife and children were brought to Gravesend by his elder brother who had bought a house next door to
his own, so that the two families could live side-by-side. Soon
Arjan was making a good wage and was able to buy a neighbouring house for his brother-in-law, whom he sponsored along
with the in-laws from Punjab. The English were selling their
houses cheaply on Kent Road, as they feared the devaluation
of property values in the light of the Punjabi influx.

The Gravesindian population explosion occurred at this time.
The increased immigration of women and children created a
more balanced society. Traditional community stability was
enhanced by families establishing themselves in houses or flats
near relatives and village-mates—thus entire kin groups lived
on the same street and dominated an entire neighbourhood.
The following case helps in understanding the development of
immigrant enclaves.

Pier Road borders Gravesend and the neighbouring town of Northfleet. It dead-ends on the River Thames, and is one of the older elite
sections of town, which, until the Punjabis moved in in 1950, was
inhabited by English old-timers. Only half the Punjabi homes on Pier
Road are kinfolk, but since they are relatives of Ajit Singh, it appears
as though the whole street is related.[1]

In 1950, Baljit Singh of Serai Khas came to Gravesend accompanied
by his wife's cousin (*chacha*'s son), Prakash Singh of Dhanowali, and
his wife's nephew, Ajit Singh of Manko. Prakash Singh's father had
been living in Gravesend since 1949, and with him, Baljit Singh and
Prakash Singh bought the house at 48 Pier Road. They lived as
bachelors there with Ajit Singh until 1952, when Baljit Singh's
brother, Sital Singh, arrived. At that time two English sisters in
number 76, moving out to the country, sold their house to Baljit Singh
and Sital Singh. When elderly Mrs Johnson migrated to Canada to

be with her daughter, Sital Singh bought number 78 from her and moved with his family into the house, along with his wife's cousin and his wife. Thus began a take-over of Pier Road by Punjabis. As they moved in, their English neighbours moved out, leaving yet another house for a Punjabi family.

When house number 79 was bought by Mrs Baljit Singh's brother, the inhabitants of number 80 could not tolerate it. They immediately sold their house to a Hindu family which had just arrived in Gravesend. The Englishman in number 77 panicked because he was surrounded by immigrants and put his house up for sale. Sital Singh, owner of number 78 and brother of Baljit Singh of number 76, could not pass up the opportunity and bought the house at a nominal price, which he then rented to fellow Punjabis. When a rift developed with his wife's cousin, Sital Singh himself moved into number 77. Baljit Singh found out that Mr Smith of number 75 was moving to Lancashire. He called his wife's sister's husband, Om Singh, and told him about the deal. Om Singh and his family moved into number 75.

Mrs Baljit Singh's brother's three sons and their uncle were staying with them when number 23 down the street went up for sale. They pooled their resources and, with Baljit Singh's help, bought the house. Mrs Baljit Singh's sister's brother and two nephews bought number 74, and their friends bought number 91. Except for 80 Pier Road, all the Punjabi families were related. When the family in number 91 discovered that number 65 was being sold, they helped their cousins buy the house.

The residential pattern remained stable until the English owners of numbers 69 and 70 sold their houses to two Indian families. The owner of number 72 sold his house to a Punjabi family because he had no English neighbours. The old lady in number 71 utterly disliked her Indian neighbourhood, but could not afford to move. Numbers 21, 24, 26, 59, 85, 86, and 93 are also owned by Punjabi families, but they are not related to Baljit Singh and Ajit Singh. Mrs Baljit Singh's brother, who lives with his sons in number 51, bought number 44 and converted it into four flats which are rented out to fellow Punjabis. Similarly, number 41, also converted into flats, is owned by Prakash Singh of number 48.

When a house in their neighbourhood is for sale, Indians immediately inform interested friends and relatives. As Indians move in and the English move out, the real estate value depreciates. This makes it easier for other Punjabis to buy the houses which are not only being sold at low prices, but are also available for immediate occupancy.

When the Gravesindian population was predominantly male, there were three Punjabi centres in operation in the older sections of Gravesend—Wakefield Street, Cutmore Street, and Pier Road—and another was growing in the neighbouring Denton and Peacock Street areas (see Figure 4). With the rapid influx, these older centres became dominated by Punjabis, while other Gravesindians stayed in the marginal areas of Darnley Road, The Avenue, and Old Road west. Living on busy streets and proximity to the town centre were given prime importance, so that both men and women could walk to stores, work, or be near a bus stop and/or railway station. Thus the Punjabis tended to settle in clusters, staying close to their own kin or village-mates when possible. Some estate agents had sold houses to Gravesindians in areas the salesmen knew were designated for future urban renewal. Shortly after moving, the immigrant family received official notice of condemnation and a meagre remuneration would be given for their substantial investment.

The influx was so sudden that within a couple of years Gravesindia rose from a little over a hundred men living in a few rooming houses in the slums to a community of several thousand scattered, but visible, Punjabis. This influx frightened some English people who were unprepared for such a seemingly permanent migrant situation.

Initially it was not the difference of race and colour that concerned the average English citizen who came in contact with these new arrivals. It was the fact that he did not appreciate what he perceived as happening to his cherished neighbourhood. To him, strange people with odd customs were flooding his locality, making him feel like a stranger in his own neighbourhood where he had been raised. These newcomers painted their doors and window frames in gaudy colours and, horror of horrors, dug up age-old rose gardens. Overcrowding, by British standards, was also a thing that appalled the Gravesindian's neighbour. Seeing ten to forty villagers living in a three-bedroom house which he considered room enough for only four or five individuals was disconcerting. Also he felt the émigré had lowered the property value of his house.

These tensions were supported by a lack of knowledge about the situation and Jat culture. For example, the Indians were

5

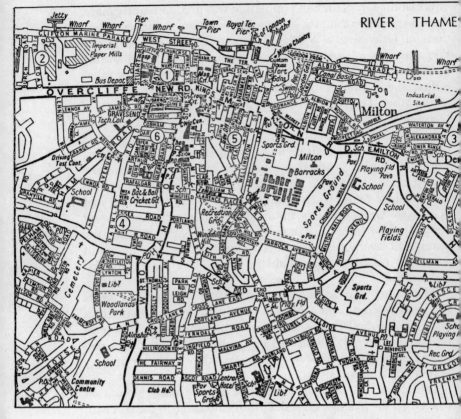

Figure 4. Indian Settlement in Gravesend

1. Wakefield Street area (the location of Bhajan Singh's guest house); it is now a car parking place
2. Pier Road area
3. Denton area (sparser immigrant settlements to the east are not shown)
4. The Avenue and Old Road West area
5. Peacock Street area
6. Cutmore Street area where Bhuta Singh had his rooming house

not able to get adequate accommodation or loans from the Council and building societies to avail themselves of better living conditions. Thus they were forced to live in overcrowded conditions or in the poorer sections of the community. In fairness, however, it must be pointed out that to the Gravesindian of that time, privacy was not known, and having only one or two people sleeping in a room was considered a waste of valuable space. So, when a Jat saw an elderly English lady living by herself in a house, he could not understand why she did not have lodgers, for there were so many of his friends and relatives who would gladly rent and provide her with extra income. To these immigrants, living together was the life-style of their village, and although crowding was not practised by them at home to the extent that it was in Gravesend, they did not mind the congestion. Later, concepts of crowding and privacy changed, but living together was accepted during this time.

Concerning the lowering of property values, this again was subject to much misunderstanding. The Punjabis did not lower property values, but it was the estate agents who perpetuated this myth. Thanks to the Sikh influx, the salesman talked the older resident into selling his house at a low price and in turn sold it at a much higher sum to an Indian family. In fact the Punjabi generally improved the condition of the house he bought, even though he did not live according to British middle-class expectations. Again, the Englishman, for instance, did not realize that the Punjabis were growing vegetables—much more important to the villager than roses—and that the possibly disagreeable odour was not a dirty smell; it was the aroma of heavy spices used in Asian cooking which could be detected by a Britisher several houses away. And it was a language barrier and a cultural reserve which inhibited friendships and neighbourliness from developing. The frugal life of the Jats was not conducive to spending money on such luxuries as rugs, baths, or new cookers. The house was a mere shelter until the family accumulated wealth and could return rich and prosperous to Punjab.

The influx of Punjabis to Gravesend resulted in a joint residence pattern[2] where more than one married couple and their children lived in a house. In 1971, 70 per cent of the approximately 300 homes of Gravesindians on the voter registration list were jointly occupied. The percentage was even higher in the earlier days. Overcrowding was quite common and had considerable advantages, since many expenses were the same whether one person or twenty lived in the house, and sharing minimized the burden on each wage-earner. Joint residence also enabled more members to bring in a wage. All children were left in the care of one grandmother, thus enabling others to work. Also joint residence brought in much more information, for five or six working members of a family were more likely to hear of better-paying jobs than only one or two.

The presence of whole families caused Gravesindians to live a life closer to that of the home village. Social relationships, formerly ignored, were reinstated, and the temporarily egalitarian society of the early years disappeared. Hierarchical evaluation and positioning, following criteria similar to those of the village, were resumed. The following situation reveals the resurfacing of caste attitudes.

Devinder, a Chamar, gained political prominence in Gravesindia among the young adults. Although they accepted his modern ideas like the abolition of the caste system and existing discrimination, he was still a Chamar and of low caste to the village Jats. Generally, when Dev entered a Jat home, the head of the house became nervous, and uneasy whispers went through the house, 'the Chamar is here'. Other low-caste individuals were not as successful as Dev, and complained about the Jats treating them as inferiors. This picture was very different from that of a group of men in the earlier days sharing rooms and beds as they sought to attain common goals. Different, too, was the re-emergence of social controls and the awareness of deviant behaviour.

The old concerns of family izzat in obtaining suitable marriage partners for offspring also came to the fore. The emigrants once again came under the same constraints as individuals living in the village. The young daughter of one of the early families described the change:

In the early years before hordes of Punjabis arrived, my mother dressed us in clothes like English children. My brothers and I associated with English friends. As our parents did not want us to be different in any way, they assured our learning the language properly.

When our relatives came, everything changed drastically. The women would come to our house and say, 'Don't you think Nimi's hair should be braided now that she is ten', or 'Nimi should not go to school with bare legs, otherwise she will grow up being immodest.' Immediately my mother's attitude changed. I was no longer to be like the English, but was to dress and be like the Punjabi villagers, whom I began to abhor.

The émigré wife was most affected if izzat was diminished. If she did not prove to be an upright wife and mother, improving the position of her husband's family, then shame would be brought on her, her parents, and kin group, as well as on her husband's family. Since women had this dual responsibility, it was they who reinstituted social control. They exerted pressure in two ways: they influenced the behaviour of their family in England, and they reinstated a full network of communication with Jandiali. These actions warrant closer examination.

The women in Gravesend pressurized their husbands into dealing with men who manifested deviant behaviour. As the following situation illustrates, this sometimes meant that husbands were admonished to withdraw their support from a man who behaved improperly. For example, Surinder Singh had been unfaithful to his wife in India by living with a white girl in England. He was once in trouble with the British police for a minor offence, and later accused of a crime he never committed. Surinder was innocent of the crime, and the Punjabi community knew it, but no one came to his defence, because the womenfolk felt it served him right to be punished in one way or another. So Surinder Singh went to jail.

Although men associated among themselves, their companions had usually to be approved of by their wives. If a woman did not like a particular associate of her husband's or did not get along with his friend's wife, she did her utmost to end the friendship. For instance, before Ram Singh's and Gobind Singh's wives came to England, they were like brothers, drinking, living, and associating with the same crowd. But because their wives, who came from Jandiali, quarrelled in the kitchen, criticized the children's behaviour, and could not get along, the two men parted company. Ram Singh and his family moved out, and these two men, who had been the best of friends, seldom, if ever, spoke to each other.

If the wife had more kinsmen in England than her husband, she exerted far greater authority and power in the family. Pritam Kaur exemplifies this. Her husband and she were sponsored and looked after by her brothers. Her husband had no kinsmen in England, so he had to concede to many more of her demands because it was her family who had given him this new opportunity. One night after he mistreated her, he had to face the wrath of her brothers and other kinfolk. She had immediately called for their assistance. Although wives without kinsmen in England were not as powerful, even lonely wives could exert considerable influence in family affairs.

The women also established a communication network between Gravesend and Jandiali. Since they had more time to write, they informed sisters in the village sending tales of jobs and behaviour of people—especially those they did not like. There were no more secrets. Communication barriers were broken, and men could no longer glorify their positions and activities. Word was quickly sent back about an individual being a 'sweeper in a factory' rather than 'an employee at Bowaters'. If a man was unfaithful to his wife, drinking excessively, or otherwise behaving improperly, news soon reached the wife or parents.

The information of the communication network also meant that the Gravesindians could no longer be strangers to one another. They knew details about each other's salaries, family, caste, degree of faithfulness to the spouse, personal habits, bank accounts, and social ranking in the home village. Having contacts in various cities and villages, it was possible to learn as much as desired about a fellow migrant. The migrant's awareness of the tightness of the network is exemplified by the dilemma of one Punjabi girl who desperately wanted to marry a boy out of caste, but deeply feared her family's wrath. Her English girl-friend suggested that she emigrate to Canada or the United States. She replied, 'There are Punjabi Jats in Canada and the United States. There is no escaping from our people!' The social networks of the Jandiali migrants were not limited to those in Gravesend; the group now widened to include those in Canada, the United States, the Philippines, and elsewhere.

I, too, experienced the tightness of the network. The Gravesindians soon had extensive knowledge not only of my work but my family background. Because of the confidence of some key members of the Gravesindian community, word spread throughout Gravesend that a joint effort should be made to assist in this study. The second experience was a little more disconcerting.

We had been in Gravesend about three weeks. The only information we had given about my wife that was that she was a Punjabi, born in Lahore, whose family was living in New Delhi. One evening at dinner the purpose of the invitation was revealed to us when the big sardar said to my wife. 'Sister Usha, you have a brother-in-law who is a high official for the State Trading Corporation.' My wife nodded affirmatively as we both sat wondering how he had obtained this information. 'We need two Austin cars in India for a taxi service, I am sure that he would be able to arrange it for extra remuneration.' We had a hard time convincing him that Usha had not seen her family for seven years and did not know how to proceed in this matter.

To this day, it is not known exactly how this Jat discovered Usha's background in so short a time. It is not difficult, however, to guess the generalities. Someone must have written to a contact in New Delhi, who was able to discover these facts. Such contacts are easily found because of the exogamous nature of village marriages; almost always someone's wife knows someone or has a relative who can obtain the desired information. Gravesindians knew practically everything about their fellow Doabans, but it generally took longer to obtain details about those from Ludhiana, Amritsar, and other areas. The explanation is simply that the vast majority of Gravesindians were from Doaba.

The re-establishment of the communication network between the Gravesindian and Jandiali Punjabi communities had other implications. The migrants in England lost their freedom from village control in several ways. First, the behaviour of a migrant could more directly affect the honour of his kinsmen in Jandiali. Yogendra Singh experienced the negative effect this could have. Although his young son in England was reasonably good about sending money home, word came back that he was drinking excessively and associating with western women and being unfaithful to his loyal wife. The whole village now knew that Yogendra's son was notorious in England, and Yogendra was

shamed in the eyes of his village-mates. They said little to him,
some even sympathized, but, nevertheless, it was agreed he had
not raised a proper son. Yogendra immediately wrote to his
brother in Birmingham to see if he could persuade his deviant
son to reform, using force if necessary.

The effect could also operate in another direction. A Punjabi
Doaban in India remarked about Bhajan Singh, whose English
accomplishments have previously been noted:

Oh, Bhajan Singh, he is nothing. His family in Jandiali is poor and
owns merely five acres of land. They have never amounted to anything, and although he has helped his family since he went to England,
they are still nothing; his brother, Mohan, is a known drunk and does
not even work.

Whether in England or in Punjab, prestige was evaluated col-
lectively for the whole family, not just for individual members.

A second effect of increased communications was that a rift
between two families in one community was reflected in the
other. Pal Singh and Gurdev Singh from Jandiali had a serious
disagreement while in Gravesend. When Pal was visiting home,
he saw to it that his younger brother discontinued his relationship with Gurdev's younger brother, thus severing the age-
long bond of friendship between the two families. Usually no
authority had to be exerted; a conflict in one community
automatically meant separation along kin lines in the other.

Third, family positions took the form common in the village.
The eldest male, whether in Jandiali or Gravesend, had greater
knowledge of the behaviour of those over whom he had authority. With this knowledge he could, and did, reassert control.
Family relations in Gravesindia were basically the same as
those in Jandiali. An elderly father might give his pay cheque
to his younger son who had migrated before him, realizing that
the son was better equipped to handle finances in England. But
it was the father who chastised his son for any deviancy.

Women regained traditional power. Punjabi women could
not speak a word of English but became a major source of
information for their husbands; elderly village ladies learned of
and relayed information about the best ways to take advantage
of income-tax loopholes or means to circumvent immigration
authorities in England. They acquired this knowledge from

shopkeepers, other women, and from fellow Gravesindians. They learned about life styles in England and the best ways to shop for bargains. They were not just housewives tending pre-schoolers, but sources and evaluers of information for their families.

In family businesses, the wife often kept the accounts, determined prices, and generally organized the business. Kewal Singh and his wife illustrate this, for they opened a haberdashery for Punjabis in Gravesend, and it was she who really ran the store. True, Kewal Singh went to the wholesalers to buy merchandise, made deliveries, and openly transacted all the business. But behind the scenes, his wife was in control. She kept the books and told him what prices to charge and to which customers; she told him how much to pay for the merchandise, and if it cost more than that, he was not to buy it. By visiting other friends and relatives, she knew the community and prices. She was the collector of information and behind-the-scenes manager for the family business.[3]

The Punjabi Sikh Jat migrant family was organized so that the most capable individuals could perform those roles for which they were best suited. As in Jandiali, no one's talents were wasted. As soon as the children attending British schools learned English, they became interpreters for their parents, relatives, and family friends.

Recalling the social changes that the immigration influx had on the Gravesend and Jandiali communities, we may say that social relationships became almost identical in both places. Although the two groups were geographically separated, they were socially united, mutually affecting, controlling, and supporting one another.

Punjabi cultural concepts of *seva, muhabbat,* and *khidmat* took on a new form with increased immigration. Initially a Punjabi in England found a room and a job for a recent arrival. Now it became necessary for Gravesindians to help one another buy homes and establish themselves, especially since they could not get mortgages. At that time, English companies were hesitant to loan money to the Punjabis, and the more established Indian families helped the younger men bring their families and successfully relocate. For example, after Mohan Singh's family arrived, he realized that the flat he was renting was not going to work out, so he approached his friend, Rajinder Singh, and explained the situation, adding, 'Rajinder, I must buy a house for my family and need to borrow some money.' Rajinder gave Mohan his cheque book and said, 'Here is my cheque book; write your own cheque, anything under four thousand pounds, for that is all I have.' Mohan Singh's case was by no means a unique one. Such loans were not made indiscriminately. Since the new arrival came from the same area, they accurately gauged family standing, which acted as a kind of collateral. Later, Mohan was reprimanded by another friend, who thought Mohan had considered Rajinder the closer friend and thus borrowed the money from him. Such mutual help, or *seva*, was common. The money was loaned with neither interest nor pressure to repay. However, there was a relationship established where either man would help the other in time of need. A man's honour was the assurance that he would eventually make good his debts. Such service, provided willingly, correlated with the cultural concepts of *muhabbat* and *khidmat*.

Non-Jats also speak very highly of Jat hospitality, like that experienced by Jarnail Singh, for when he arrived in England from Ludhiana City, he had two pounds in his pocket. While walking the streets, he met a Jat family who took him in and looked after him until he found a job and settled down. 'You know, they would not take anything for food and lodging provided to me during those three months', he told me over a pint of beer; 'I think we sophisticated people have lost something in our education which these simple villagers still have.'

Seva to others afforded *robh* and izzat; however, there was another kind of *seva* and that was informing a kinsman or village-mate in Jandiali of the unacceptable behaviour of, for example, a son. Since an errant son could endanger his family's position, one was serving his parents by making it possible for them to influence the son to change before it became too late or too damaging.

Political ambition also gained prominence during the middle period. The gurdwara became the arena for political competition, and alliances shifted to those cultural brokers who did not exploit Punjabis and who now acquired the title of 'social worker'. The following description is of one such man.

Surinder Singh came to Gravesend around 1960. He knew

both English and Punjabi, and used his knowledge to help others. Surinder had completed two years of college at a school in Punjab and was able to decipher the complicated forms relating to social service benefits. When a man was injured in the factory, Surinder helped him with his applications for compensation. When a friend needed to enroll his daughter in school, Surinder went along to help out. Although others in the community performed these brokerage functions for a fee or to gain political power, Surinder Singh was a true social worker—he served for the benefit of the community. When Surinder's name was nominated for the position of gurdwara secretary, he declined. 'I am a weak man,' he explained later; 'I am from Majha, not Doaba; I have no relatives here to support me.'

The social worker did not ask for remuneration for his services, but performed tasks as one friend for another. As a result, a loyal following developed around these helpful individuals who had the potential for political leadership, but, as in Surinder's case, they could never be as powerful as those who had a core of kinsmen backing them at all costs during times of need.

The gurdwara was not only a religious house, but the political arena for communal strife. This latter use was not surprising, because the leaders of gurdwaras, both in India and abroad, controlled considerable sums of money, and gurdwara authorities represented the community to the British authorities in most phases of Sikh life. Furthermore, with the influx of more people, the Gravesend gurdwara grew in importance and became a primary social centre. Gravesindians took gurdwara politics seriously, and vied for the position of president. Also the gurdwara was a symbol of Sikhism. It had the same significance as a national flag or church. It was a symbol of unity for all the Gravesindians, Sikhs and non-Sikhs. Thus, being a gurdwara president carried considerable prestige in its own right.

This middle period also saw roles within the family becoming more specialized, thus increasing efficiency in a joint residence as the following case explains.

In Rattan Singh's household, all available members helped to enhance the family's resources. He worked in construction, not as steady as factory work, but Rattan Singh had learned that despite the irregular hours, he could make more money on construction than his counter-part in the factory. Rattan Singh had obtained a job for his eldest son and they worked side-by-side.

Rattan Singh's wife and daughter-in-law worked at the Bata Shoe Factory. They both left the house every morning around 6 a.m. His mother cared for the children while they were gone. Rattan Singh's wife, however, was still in charge of the kitchen and cooked large quantities of food at night for the following day. Rattan Singh's father worked at Bowaters. He looked young, and by claiming a younger age, he was able to get a satisfactory job.

Since Rattan Singh knew English and was the first to come to England, he was most familiar with English ways. All earning members of the family automatically turned their pay cheques over to him and he faithfully deposited the five pay cheques bi-weekly. Each member received some pocket money, and decisions for major expenditure were made by family consensus. As always, the women had a strong say.

At night after the men came home from the pub, they shared what they had done or learned during the day. The women were around and participated, but they did not eat with the men. Their contribution was given later, and their gossip and ideas were always accepted.

Rattan Singh's family was quite typical. They opted for those jobs that were not relished by the English. Construction was such an area, for the English mostly preferred regular and more secure jobs. By specialization within the household, more money could be earned. The grandmother cared for the children and became the family tactician and a collector of community gossip. All other adults worked and gathered information, and the most capable member of the family—in this case, Rattan Singh—handled the finances. But, as head of the household, the grandfather represented the family at *akhand paths* and other rituals.

The pooling of resources, which was common in most families, made large amounts of money readily available for lucrative investment opportunities, thus avoiding finance charges and interest rates. This joint economy also worked well at an international level. If a brother in Hong Kong perceived a business opportunity, his brothers in England, the United States, and Kenya would readily send him the money to start. Family assets were diversified, and any member who failed knew that he would be bailed out by his kinsmen.

This family organization was like the family firm. Benedict (1968) argues that such family firms are advantageous; they have diversity of income, pooled capital, and thus can take greater risks. Communication in the firm is informal and yet more efficient, giving the group greater flexibility. Besides, the participants are more loyal and have a greater incentive to work hard. These characteristics enabled the Gravesindian to be more solvent than his British counterpart, even though his home and life-style did not reveal this extra wealth.

In pursuing joint economic security, the Gravesend–Jandiali migrants adopted two other tactics: attainment of a sophisticated (although narrow) understanding of English political, economic, and legal systems; and assuming a very flexible attitude vis-à-vis employment. Nearly all Gravesindians were aware of their situation in England. They knew which stores to trade with; they were also familiar with, and knew how best to use welfare benefits and medical services. The Punjabis did not forcefully try to change their station in British society, but were concerned with how the laws and rules were applied and how to manipulate them.

Concerning economic flexibility, it has already been noted that the Sikh Jat went where money or jobs were available—anywhere in the world. Gravesindians, both men and women, commuted to the other side of London to work, while most of their English counterparts preferred jobs in Gravesend. Other Punjabi men left their families in Gravesend and went to Birmingham or Bedford to live with a brother or friend while they worked on a new job or hunted for one. If things worked out, they brought their families. If a brother told of opportunities in the United States, a man willingly gave it a try, bringing his family later if all went well. Family ties or regional loyalties did not prohibit the Punjabi from leaving everything to seek his fortune.

The Gravesindians' continued obsession with making money brought other changes. Punjabis in England worked much harder than they did in the village. One man commented:

When I worked one job, I had too much free time to visit the pub. Generally in the evening I was restless because we Jats are unhappy unless we are working hard. So I started this grocery delivery business in my spare time.

It seems that working in a factory for long hours became a symbol of manliness; men were proud of their ability to put in longer hours than their English counterparts. They spoke freely of this ability.

In the foundry where I worked, there were mostly Punjabis employed because we were strong and could endure the heavy labour and extreme heat. Not only that, but we could stay on the job for several shifts, which is more than the English could do![4]

The man who lost his job, however, was a sad case. He could collect unemployment insurance, but he lost his pride. He looked hard for employment, fearing his position in the home would be usurped by his working wife. Sher Singh, for instance, injured his leg at the Ford plant. Even though this was not a serious handicap, it prohibited him from doing the heavy work his job required, and he was on welfare. His wife, in the meantime, worked on a farm picking vegetables. Sher Singh no longer held his head high, for his wife was earning a better income than he. But, worst of all, she was working and he was not. She started usurping more authority in the house, for she now provided for the family. He looked after the children or saw friends when the younger ones were in school. But Sher Singh's pride was ebbing, for he no longer was the breadwinner.

Not only did men work long hours, but some women held two or more jobs. Almost all working wives had at least one other job, that of assisting in the family business, along with household duties of cooking, cleaning, and looking after the family. As the Gravesindians tended to regard their situation as temporary, their awareness that such opportunities and work were unavailable in the village made them work harder to earn more as rapidly as possible.

If and when there were no elderly women to tend the young children, a grave problem arose. During these middle years and into the 1970s, Gravesend authorities faced the problem of very young Punjabi children being left home alone while both parents worked. Punjabi parents were notorious for leaving three- and four-year-olds locked in the house with a sandwich, biscuits, and a flask of tea. Cases of burns have been cited by nurses and hospital authorities. The norm, however, was to have one member of the residence group watch all the children, cook, and look after the house while everyone else worked. As soon as was possible, around the age of fifteen, sons went off to work in their fathers' factories and daughters joined their mothers.

With the arrival of families in Gravesindia, male life-styles underwent a change. Although the pub continued to be the social centre for most men, and the place of work as conducive for discussion and debate, some social activities began to shift to the home. In the living room, friends and party members gathered to converse about local issues and to plan political strategy. Men were always afforded priority here; the womenfolk generally congregated in the kitchen, cooking and visiting each other. Some Gravesindian homes had the television in the living room, whereas others had it in the back room next to the kitchen for the children and ladies. 'Telly' was considered extremely important as a source for learning English and Punjabis delighted in soap operas and wrestling.

Besides being the focal place for political manoeuvre, the Gravesend gurdwara also developed into a social centre. Here the Gravesindian community met as a unit to discuss problems. Sundays became very important for these Sikhs in England, for men in their best suits with their gaily dressed women and brightly clothed children headed for their place of worship when the services started. Women always sat to the right of the Granth Sahib and the men on the left, facing its canopy. As in later years, devout men constantly complained of the noise from the female sector, where the whisper of gossip turned into a loud mumble that sometimes drowned out the speaker; children, crying and shouting freely, added to the confusion. The gurdwara committee at one time assigned key men to police the women's side, but to no avail; for most women, the gurdwara was their only weekly outing.

The early 1960s saw little, if any, change in the previous English attitude toward the Punjabis, although anti-immigrant sentiment was evident against other communities. However, there was a definite change among the Punjabis, who openly taught their children not to emulate or associate with the English. Mothers pressured one another to make their daughters uphold Punjabi traits, to keep their hair braided and legs covered. Early marriages were arranged before the young adults became attracted to western girls.

Separation from the English was widely instituted. The migrants did not want their members to adopt the seemingly immoral sexual behaviour of the host group. The British system of co-education deeply worried the Punjabis, who did not approve of their girls associating with boys. Gravesindians were Punjabis first, and continued to define their social position in opposition to their hosts. The arrival of the women accentuated these feelings, and the Punjabis chose to remain separate.

Gravesindia and Jandiali become one community

The home village for the Gravesindians increasingly became the group to imitate and evaluate themselves by; village cultural principles were reintroduced and enforced. Besides making money to enhance the family's honour, one had to also live according to the dictates of Punjabi Sikh Jat culture and uphold that family's honour. Children were coerced to be Punjabis and to remain distinctive. Punjabi Sikh Jat men were no longer free, as they had been, to associate with English girls, and their wives made sure restrictions were placed on male behaviour. An England-returnee did not enjoy automatically the high status he once had, although the emigrant's own self-image was one of superiority. As one villager said, 'They are just common labourers in the factory, working like dogs, while I am a king on my land.' Villagers soon realized that behaviour in England was below their standards and that going to England was not what they had visualized. In spite of this, the exodus of men, women, and children from Jandiali continued, leaving their land in the custody of a friend or relative. The fear that entry to Britain would be closed was the greatest motivating factor for this mass outflow.

Although some repulsive aspects of English behaviour were known to the Punjabis prior to emigration, elaborate details in the middle years increased the concern of the elders. The village became the group of evaluation in this period, and this intensified as time went on.

With the influx of the 1960–2 period, the communications networks of Jandialians in England and Punjab developed so efficiently that Gravesindians could no longer escape the watchful eye of their village counterparts. Geographical distance did not inhibit the social evaluation of one's kin and village-mates thousands of miles away. Also, the arrival of women had laid the basis for enforcing Punjabi cultural norms, both in Gravesend and in the village.

The joint family and extended kin group of the Punjabis gave them a tremendous economic advantage over their English competitors in accumulating capital and obtaining employment. Thus, it was not long before the host community began to wonder how these Asians got their wealth—possibly leading to the English feeling that Indians were exploiting the social services. However, peace in Gravesend was not to last forever, and the Jats were soon to face a harsh decision as to the future—their own and that of their progeny.

CHAPTER VI

STAYING LONGER
(1963-1971)

Permanent settlement becomes plausible

The situation changed for the Gravesend–Jandiali migrant group for they not only had to adapt to the changing political and economic situation of Britain but, as this chapter indicates, they had to deal with intra-community tensions as well. Concerning the wider context in which the Gravesindians were living, the passage of the 1962 Bill concerning immigration was 'obviously discriminatory' (Steel 1969: 47). Also, there was a concern that huge numbers of Kenyan Asians would invade Britain. Frank McLeavy, MP for Bradford, summed up British sentiment when he said 'we cannot afford to be the welfare state for the whole Commonwealth.' Many Englishmen, especially blue-collar workers, wrongly assumed that West Indians and Asians were taking their jobs. This resulted in anti-immigrant feeling being strongest amongst that segment of the population. Consequently, immigration was a much larger issue in the 1964 campaign than it had been previously, and the Indian Workers' Association had formed a liaison with the Labour Party—making Asian views known and also helping their allies maintain some of their seats.

This wider situation was reflected in Gravesend for the back issues of the *Gravesend Reporter* showed that 1963 was a crucial period in terms of Anglo-Sikh relations. Some pubs began refusing service to coloureds; racist letters protesting against alien infiltration appeared on the editor's desk, and local politicians had to face hostile constituents. The election of Kundan 'Kim' Bhojwani,[1] a Sindhi from Karachi, as Vice-Chairman of the Gravesend Liberal Association (membership included sixty Indians and twenty British) marked the beginning of direct action by Indian politicians in voicing the concerns of their fellow countrymen.

In 1964, ugly incidents began to occur in the Gravesend area. One such event concerned a turbaned school teacher and his family who were given Council housing.[2] The hostile white neighbours damaged the Sikh teacher's property by breaking windows, slashing car tyres, and shouting obscenities at the women and children. The family was forced to move out into an Indian neighbourhood. Although not as violent as in other places, discrimination against the Punjabi community in Gravesend was present. Generally, it was more subtle, like a nudge on the street or a clerk not waiting on an Indian in an English-owned business. But the Gravesindian had more pressing problems—bringing other family members to England, relieving family tensions, and dealing with unscrupulous exploiters.

These new problems faced by the Gravesindians were partly caused by the new categories of Indian immigrants. The arrival of old parents, for instance, brought family tensions within the joint unit which were not previously felt. The voucher system,[3] instituted by the British government in 1962, curbed the inflow of villagers but increased the proportion of educated urbanites who too had their own problems of adjustment.

In the case of the elderly, their influx was instituted by emotional appeals from parents, pressuring their sons and relatives to sponsor them to England. Parents coerced doctors in India to write letters of a serious illness that would force their sons to send for them.

Upon arrival, the elderly migrants became a part of the Gravesindian community. The physically strong, able-bodied old men lied about their age and became a vital part of the work force, taking on heavy construction work along with the younger men, thus aiding in increasing family assets. The elder women contributed by tending children, cooking and keeping house, thus freeing one more individual to bring in a pay cheque.

The reaction of Gobind Singh's parents is an apt illustration of the happenings of this time. After Gobind Singh had been in England for a short time, he brought his wife and children to Gravesend. Soon after his dependents' arrival, he began re-

ceiving letters from Punjab telling him of the failing health of
his mother. Being the only son, Gobind held a special place in
her heart. The letters, however, wrote of her broken heart, how
she missed her grand-children whom she had loved so dearly.
Shortly thereafter, a doctor in Punjab wrote to Gobind saying
his mother was dying of a broken heart—sadness was killing
her. If he loved his mother, he should either return to Punjab
or take her to England. Gobind's sister also wrote to him
requesting that he sponsor his mother and father.

Relations between Gobind's wife and mother had not been
good. There had been tension between them from the beginning. But, considering all the circumstances, Gobind's wife
consented and even encouraged him to bring his so-called
dying mother to England. Gobind brought his parents to England. Her psychosomatic illness was quickly cured. Even though
he was 70 years old, Gobind's father obtained a construction
job, and his mother, who was not able to get a job, managed the
children, thus freeing Gobind's wife for work at the Bata Shoe
Company.

Any animosity that may previously have existed between the
wife and mother-in-law in Punjab was greatly intensified in
England. Both women competed for high status, affection, and
loyalty of the youngsters. The wife further contested against
the mother-in-law for her husband's attention. It did not take
long for an elderly Punjabi woman in England to realize that
she did not have the secure position she had in Punjab. In the
village, as the seniormost woman, as owner of the house and/or
land, she was the matriarch; but coming to England she soon
realized that her son's wife had assumed that position and
jealously guarded it. Although due respect was accorded to the
elders, they were guests. In this position, they did not have the
authority they held when they brought their son's bride to their
Jandiali home. Hence, it is no surprise that the elderly Gravesindian woman feared that if something happened to her
husband, she would be at the mercy of her son and his wife,
who might turn her out of the house and, like the westerners,
put old people in 'living graves'.[4] Her only solace was in her
grand-children whom she spoiled and her fellow Punjabis,
whom she hoped would pressure her son to look after his
mother. This was even more so for Jat families with only one

son; there was greater security when there were two or more boys to share the burden of the aged.

The great insecurity for the elderly migrant mother in England stemmed from two factors: first, her age precluded employment, and secondly her previous position as absolute matriarch was usurped by her daughter-in-law. The latter had experienced privacy and ran her own household without her mother-in-law's interference. She resented the old lady's spoiling her utopia. As one lady put it:

Mohan Singh and I had a beautiful relationship; we loved each other deeply, had two sons within two years, and worked together as a team. Our children were happy as we enjoyed a family life. Then, that old witch [mother-in-law] had to come and spoil everything. We now have family fights, and I am once again treated shabbily, while they all, including Mohan, gang up against me.

The mother wanted her son to be obliged to her, because his wife desired her to leave. She was also unsure of whom her son would side with if and when a choice arose. Therefore, the elderly woman began to cultivate an extremely close relationship with her grand-children; she loved them, coddled them, slept with them, and provided love when they were disciplined, but never chastised them herself. This grandmother–grandchild relationship was similar to that in Punjab, but because of the insecurity, it was greatly intensified in Gravesindia. An example is that of *Bébé* Pritam Kaur who was being sent back to Punjab because of constant quarrels with her daughter-in-law. Her grand-children opposed this so vociferously that she finally stayed in England, much to the chagrin of their mother. The old lady had instilled in her grand-children that she would die if she was separated from them. Besides that, the children were used to sleeping with their *Bébé* and could not bear to part with her.

The daughter-in-law was also at a disadvantage in this game of vying for affection. She worked all day away from home, while the 'old lady' stayed in the house and influenced her children. One bright young woman from Doaba who was extremely harrassed by her mother-in-law remarked,

Bébé is perfectly capable of looking after my children during the day, even carrying around our thirty-pound son. She claims, however, that her arthritis prohibits her from cleaning the house, washing diapers, and cooking the evening meal. I have to do all that work when I come home, so I have no time for my children. Naturally, the children love her. I know my children are being spoiled, but every time I discipline them, they run to that witch and she gives them sympathy, turning them against me.

The husband was torn between his mother and his wife; he felt obliged to obey his mother, and his unhappy wife made life miserable for him by refusing his overtures in the bedroom. It is interesting that the arrival of the elderly did not necessarily bring conservatism. They were intelligent enough to accept certain changes as long as they did not affect the family's honour. Undoubtedly, the elders had *robh* and were often called to adjudge family feuds. As in the circumstances of Shiro Kaur, one can observe that Bhajan Singh radically departed from normal Punjabi behaviour.

Shiro Kaur was one of the few girls in Punjab to go to a college. Thus, when she was brought to England by her husband, she obtained a job in a London bank and was very upset when her father-in-law demanded that she give her entire pay cheque to him. Her in-laws claimed that she showed disrespect to her mother-in-law. Although her husband's parents had come to her husband's house and she was the dominant female, they felt that she should not show her contempt so openly.

Shiro Kaur went with her problem to Bhajan Singh, who was an elder of their village, thus a natural person to settle the conflict. She explained how her husband's parents mistreated her; how they took her money and curbed her freedom. Bhajan Singh listened to Shiro Kaur's parents-in-law also, who told of how she was disrespectful to her elders and that she had been corrupted by English ways, trying to be independent rather than the demure Punjabi housewife. Bhajan Singh ruled that Shiro Kaur should be allowed to keep her own bank account, but that she should also behave more respectfully toward her husband's parents.

Bhajan Singh, however, realized that things were different in England and that changes had to be made. If leniency was not allowed, the situation could become intolerable for Shiro Kaur and her family, which might eventually bring about a split. This case also illustrates that when conflicts took place,

whether inter- or intra-family, a common elder was appealed to
for settlement. As in Jandiali, elders were considered the holders
of wisdom acquired through a lifetime of experience. A respected elder in Punjab brought that respect with him to England, and people came to him just as they would in Jandiali.

There were other reasons for the changing attitudes of the
elders. Since a son was no longer dependent upon his father for
livelihood as he would have been in Punjab, he could leave his
family and earn his own way. Younger brothers were no longer
economically dependent on older brothers. With factory jobs
readily available, one could leave home and become self-
reliant. Therefore, new means were devised to deal with these
problems. The elders, or those in authority, became less strict
with subordinates and exerted far less pressure on them. A
father often spoiled his son, sometimes giving him more than
his due share, hoping thereby to keep the family together. An
older brother was likely to grant the request of his younger
brother and listen to his ideas more attentively, hoping that the
lad would not leave the family. Pal experienced the benefits of
this fear as the younger brother in the household. Although he
was earning a good wage at the factory, he seemed to be getting
more than his share in benefits. Whenever he needed money for
beer, his mother gave it to him. Whenever his wife wanted new
clothes, she was usually allowed to spend the money. It seemed
that, although the rest of the family was on an austere budget,
Pal and his wife were living well.

This flexibility of family heads kept the joint-family system
from breaking down. Where there was no joint-residence situation, individuals preferred to live in the vicinity of their kin
groups, thus keeping intact the authoritarian relationships.
Even though it was possible for Indians to break away from the
influence of their kin group, they chose not to do so for several
reasons, one being that ties between parents and children
tended to be particularly strong. Also, growing up with kinsmen
around gave a security which a person was not willing to forgo.
Being in a foreign land where he knew about western individualism, he did not want to break away from the kin group
and relinquish its support. Living without the backing of family
and village-mates could be a traumatic experience for any
Indian.

In due time, a few Indian families learnt to manage by themselves. One such family was that of Jeevan Kaur, who came to Gravesend with her mother and younger brother at the age of four. She went through the English school system, and at six she was indispensable. She accompanied her mother to the store and post office to interpret for her, and by the age of ten she was helping her father with income-tax forms, health service applications, and anything else that required her brokerage abilities. Not only did she aid her parents, but whenever her uncles, aunts, or cousins needed her, she also assisted them. Much of her vacation from college was spent filling forms, accompanying relatives to various offices, and also advising them. Children like Jeevan Kaur made a few families free of the influence of cultural brokers. However, there were some aspects which these children could not deal with, for which the adults had to look to the cultural broker. But his influence was on the decline.

Many Gravesindian families began to take on a different form during this time—a 'split family' situation began to occur; that is, couples had two groups of children with a five-to-eight-year gap between them. The arrival of wives contributed to this population increase; for the Jandialian man felt bound to start a 'second family', that is, have more children. To him and his wife, having children demonstrated to the Gravesindian and home communities that he still cherished his spouse and would quell the fears and rumours of unfaithfulness that persisted in the village of origin. Indian parents tended to consider a marriage successful only when a bride became pregnant. If she was not with child by the first or second month of marriage, people questioned the consummation of the union, its success and potential for permanence. Upon arrival in England, most Punjabi women came with teenage children; but they became pregnant again to demonstrate to their society that loyalty was still present.

The second type of family structure, that is, a man having more than one wife, did not deviate from that practised in Punjab; but it was not advertised to the British. The situation of Lashman Singh is a very good example, for he came to England in the 1950s and brought his wife shortly thereafter. Unfortunately, twelve years elapsed and they were not blessed

Street scenes in Jandiali: local vegetable vendor (above);
enjoying sugar cane (below)

Ganda Singh (extreme right) : 90-year-old returnee

Prospective emigrants:
one member of family
already in England

Immigrant pedlars

Émigré: training
to be a nurse

Akhand path

Indian Youth Federation meeting

Punjabi field instead of rose garden: Gravesindian backyard

House sold to
Gravesindian:
The Avenue

Pukka houses and bungalows built with emigrant money

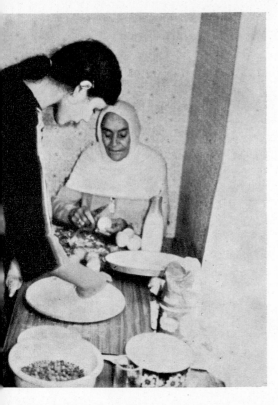

Cooking: in the
village (above);
in Gravesindia (below)

Jandiali 1978: almost a ghost village

Tube-well in Jandiali:
built with pounds sterling

with children. By 1967, both Lashman and his wife werè very sad, and he finally heeded her plea for bringing a second wife from Punjab so that his blood line could be carried down. Lashman and his two wives now have a family of several children.

Although Lashman's situation is rare, it does happen, for to the rural Jat it is imperative that his substance be continued, and it can only be done through sons. Thus, it is culturally acceptable for him to have another wife if no sons are born. Lashman's wife was sad because she could not bear her husband children; thus, she persuaded him to have another wife. Of course, being an England-returnee gave him status and wealth and he had no trouble finding a second spouse. In many instances, however, the barren wife usually arranges a match for her husband from among her kinfolk or village-mates.

In the rural Jat family, there is real love and consideration in these matters. A loving wife will want her husband to marry again. In some cases, a wife's sister will have relations with the husband, and after the child is born will give it to her childless sibling. If the problem is with the husband, a brother may sire the child. These actions, which are not taken indiscriminately or lightly, certainly demonstrate the closeness within the family of rural Punjabis.

The coming of the educated urbanites was encouraged by the voucher system, and they arrived in greater numbers. Why some of these people came is sometimes a mystery, and, as Lal Singh states, the individual may not know for sure himself:

As I worked in our family accounting firm in Phagwara, I continually heard and read newspaper stories of these ignorant villagers making fortunes in England. I learned about the voucher scheme of immigration to Britain, but I was in a good business and had no desire to move. One day while joking around in the office, several of my friends wagered that I could not gain admittance to Britain. Thus, as a joke, my wife and I applied. When we received approval from the English authorities, we were in a dilemma, for Baljinder, my wife, and I knew that we would not have the opportunity again to emigrate. We were happy in Phagwara with my brothers and family around, and we were making very good money.

Baljinder and I left for Britain on the very last day before our admittance to U.K. expired, just to see what it was like. I had the name of some friends in Birmingham who directed me to a paper testing job at the paper mill here in Gravesend. It was a lowly job—far beneath my abilities and qualifications. But I took it. I was ready to return to Punjab immediately, yet if I did, I would be regarded as a failure, and people would wonder why I had not succeeded in England where those villagers had done so well. Thus, I have stayed. After being here five years, you can see I have advanced to my present job as a government official. But if I would have stayed in Punjab, I would have done very well and been with my family. However, I could never have such a fine home in Punjab, with the nice decorations and carpeting, like I have here in England. I do want my parents to come and see the good life I lead here.

Living with these villagers is really difficult. Every night one of them is here for help with a problem having to do with the British bureaucracy. Baljinder really gets upset with me for not turning them away, for I go for weeks without a decent night's sleep. How can I refuse them when they need my assistance? Yet, living with them in Gravesend, I am not an entirely free man, either. Baljinder does not like their criticism, and has to be careful not to wear dresses or cut her hair. I would have liked to try for a police interpreter's job, but knew that it would bring reprisals on my family and me from the Jats, for they would think that I was going to try and extort from them as others have done. Besides, I have no other kinsmen here to protect me if I receive communal disfavour. It is a tight rope I walk here!

The educated Indians brought their own problems. Some came due to reasons set forth in Chapter III, while others just migrated to try out life in England, and once they arrived, were socially trapped. They were not happy in England, but did not dare return to Punjab and risk the humiliation of being considered failures. In Punjab, it was assumed that people only returned to India because they were unsuccessful in England; and Punjabi society was generally quite cruel in the subtle humiliation it inflicted on such a person, his parents, and his kin group. Therefore, many professionals continued to stay in Britain in unskilled labouring jobs rather than face the consequences of returning to India.

Since the educated immigrant was very frustrated, he was dissatisfied and most likely to register complaints about unequal treatment. Those of rural origin tended to overlook improper treatment, as life was much better abroad than in the village; and they did not necessarily want the situation altered.

The urban educated migrant had options like moving into an

English neighbourhood away from other Indians, although this had the disadvantage of not giving him the social support that his community offered, and to the Punjabi such security was essential. Plus, moving out carried the risk that a British area may not accept him. Many, however, took this option, though they led very lonely lives unless brothers and cousins moved nearby.

For those who chose to remain within the Indian sector or on the marginal areas, life was very hard. Many of the educated did a wonderful job of helping their village counterparts adjust and survive in England. School teachers tutored, ex-lawyers interpreted, doctors counselled, thus helping form an organization to promote Sikhism, Punjabi culture, or helping the community to represent themselves to local authorities. Some were recognized by the host community, while others continued to do these functions without adequate thanks being offered.

There was another Indian element that was not so altruistic. Inder Singh was an example, for he set up his one-man employment exchange and became rich by helping people obtain jobs and later by extorting and coercing those he had initially advised. He did this by telling villagers to claim more dependents in Punjab than there actually were, thus saving on income-tax. After the form was filed, he threatened to expose the aided individual unless he paid a bribe or helped in a manner Inder determined. The early Punjabi immigrant, being ignorant and fearful of English ways, easily complied. Those who were smuggled into England also had similar problems; as one Asian stated, 'If you are smuggled into England, you are never a free man again.' There were other cases of exploitation of Indians by fellow Indians. For example, Gautam Patel, who interpreted for the Gravesend police department, was later convicted for rendering false interpretations.[5] Some Gravesindians claim that when one of them was taken to the police station, this Gujrati would ask in the vernacular for twenty pounds or threaten them with conviction. The police did not know what was being said in Punjabi and the accused did not understand what was being transmitted in English. The victim was always open to extortion from this Asian policeman. The police department was apprised of this situation, but refused for several years to even consider that one of its employees might be dishonest.

Brokers from the early and middle years were generally notorious for their exploitation. The Jats were known for believing that their future was in the hands of their sons and their land, both of which would provide for them in old age. Therefore, it was surprising when Maharaj Mehra, an insurance agent, boasted extremely high sales among the Gravesindian community. On questioning, it turned out that the insurance agent had, in the earlier years, been a broker and had advised people to cheat, and now, if they did not buy insurance from him, he threatened to go to the police. The victims had no way of defending themselves against such people unless they faced jail or had kin in Gravesend to safeguard them.

The Punjabis also needed protection from the English community, since exploitation by salesmen and merchants was not uncommon. A Punjabi family purchased a sewing machine. When the machine failed to work properly, they called the shop, requesting a repairman. Three months later, a representative made a call. At that time he informed the family that their guarantee had expired the past week. To the English-speaking daughter's protest that they had called three months ago, he replied: 'Sorry about that! Now if you buy the repair insurance service we offer, we may be able to do something.' The girl told him, 'We did buy insurance, but my father is at work.' A more knowledgeable Punjabi neighbour piped in, 'Surely you have a record of their insurance at the store?' To this the repairman replied, 'Well, you know how easily such things are lost', and left after charging ten pounds for repairs.

During this period, more active discrimination began. Young English boys cornered Punjabi lads in dark alleys and beat them. Punjabi homes, where the husband worked a night-shift, were marked and the women were threatened in his absence. These episodes never made the news, and Punjabi communities reacted quietly, but efficiently. Almost every Punjabi family installed a telephone, especially households where husbands worked nights or which were in a marginal neighbourhood. Then they quickly came to the aid of each other. For example, one night a car of English boys came up to a Punjabi home and threw rocks at the window. Within minutes of a telephone call, a car of Jat men drove up and patrolled the area searching for the English culprits. The Sikhs maintained that they had to take the law into their own hands because the police did nothing to protect them. The adults travelled in pairs and instructed young boys always to associate in groups. Such group fraternities were common among the Sikh Jats and proved useful in Gravesend for self-protection.

With the increasing number of children performing the services of a cultural broker, the dominance of such men as Bhuta Singh and Bhajan Singh declined. However, the Gravesindians had to deal with extortion, from people like Mahesh Mehra and Gautam Patel, and discrimination. Parliament did pass the Race Relations Act, but the penalties were light, and its use, in the view of the Punjabis, was negligible. The transformation of the Gravesend Friendship Council into the Community Relations Council[6] provided an arena where the English and Punjabis could openly discuss problems concerning their interaction, but the need remained for some formal means of representing the Gravesindians. The Punjabis in Gravesend also wanted to promote their culture. Children were being taught English ways and traditions in the schools, while forgetting their own. They were not being reminded of the glories of Punjab and Punjab's rich tradition.

The answers to many of these problems for the Gravesindians lay in the formation of parties and organizations such as the Gurdwara Committee and the Indian Workers' Association. What the Punjabis termed a 'party'[7] operated within the framework of Indian and English organizations and helped their constituents. A party, while being sensitive to the needs of the community, sought, at the same time, to maximize its power.

Although organizations like the Gurdwara Committee were supposed to have a specific purpose, they all took on the general function of providing cultural and adaptive services for the Gravesindian community. This took the form of representing the Punjabis to the English authorities, providing cultural programmes and celebrations, and helping their constituents deal with the British bureaucracy.

It was important for the Jats to hold positions of key importance like president, secretary, and executive council members. The elected president of an immigrant organization had ultimate decision-making power, but he had to be sensitive to public opinion and implement the wishes of his constituency. If he did not, chances of returning to his position were minimized. The president picked his own committee of office bearers and advisers, usually from within his own party, with a few neutrals or weak members from the opposite group to show fairness and to combat charges of partiality. Members of the opposite party usually were given the difficult jobs, such as treasurer, so that if there were any missing funds they were the responsibility of the opposition and no charges could be made against the party in power. The president was a diplomat who consulted his stalwarts before making any final decisions and was never autocratic for fear of alienating his supporters. He was basically the symbolic head of the organization.

The secretary, on the other hand, really made the organizational machine run smoothly. He kept a list of all members of the community, handled all correspondence, and acted as liaison between the president and the constituency. Usually he contacted members and persuaded them to a certain point of view. He was a strong potential threat to the president's leadership because of his direct contact with the people which made him popular. If there was a split in the party or a quarrel among the officers, it was not unusual for the president and the secretary to be on opposite sides. Therefore, a president not only chose a capable secretary, but one who was a close associate and friend and loyal to him at all costs. This was often a difficult combination to find.

Indian associations like the Gurdwara Committee and Indian Workers' Association had an executive council composed of an odd number of members to prevent a tie vote, although decisions were generally made by consensus. Usually, able persons who served the community and were popular served on the executive council. It was often the Gurdwara Committee of each area that was recognized by the British as the mouthpiece of the Punjabi community. Gravesend boasted the largest gurdwara in England, and hence had a strong voice in race and cultural affairs. Within the framework of this organization operated the party, whose primary purpose was to gain power by controlling and ultimately representing Gravesindia to outsiders.

In the political party of the Gravesindians, there were six

identifiable roles: 'kingmaker', 'core of advisers', 'broker', 'social worker', 'sympathizer', and of course, 'member'.[8] The kingmaker usually was a former president of an organization such as the Gurdwara Committee, who, though politically strong, had made enemies. Since he did not have sufficient strength to obtain or hold office himself, his following provided a strong core of support for any candidate he chose. The king-maker himself remained in the background, supporting, advising, and determining the policy of his candidate. The Gravesindians often knew who the kingmaker was and that if his candidate won, he would have complete power. Because he worked in the background, the esteem of the kingmaker was not risked if his candidate lost the election, unless he had un-diplomatically publicized his support.

The kingmaker had a core of advisers with whom he and the president met to discuss local politics and strategy. These advisers were skilled in political activity and knew their community. Intelligent and politically able men, these advisers generally lacked sufficient relatives for a core following of their own.

Some writers[9] use the terms 'social worker' and 'broker' synonymously, but in this study they do not have the same meaning. The social worker and broker were essential to any Punjabi migrant political party or organization, and by the help afforded to others, both gained a following. The social worker selflessly helped his fellow Punjabis, whereas a broker bridged the cultural gap between the British and Punjabi communities. The latter was usually bilingual and knew enough about English ways to help people with income-tax, medical and social service forms, jobs, and general survival in Britain; but he was in a position to exploit his fellow immigrants, as Mahesh Mehra did.

Those who helped their fellow Gravesindians selflessly were called 'social workers'. Bhajan Singh of Jandiali is a good example, as he helped friends fill out forms and obtain driver's licences and/or interpreted for them at the doctor's office. Although he could not always do these services himself, he would arrange to have them done. Most social workers neither asked for anything in return nor sought political office; they simply befriended those in need. Unfortunately, the leaders of the English Gravesend community often could not differentiate between the exploiting broker and the helpful social worker, and often unknowingly aided the exploiting broker.

The sympathizer was not active in any party, but because he had friends or relatives in one, he was considered sympathetic towards that party. Since he was not actively committed to any group, he gained the confidence of both parties and mediated in case of conflict and disagreement. He was in a precarious position because one or the other party was often suspicious of him and did not always regard him as neutral.

Members aligned themselves with a party. Membership was informal, but recognizable, and kin groups seldom split. Brothers, fathers, uncles, and cousins usually belonged to the same party, as did village-mates, unless there had been an intra-village conflict.

Yet another group of Punjabis who exercised considerable influence were those who moved out while retaining various financial interests in Gravesend. They were not classifiable in any one of the above categories, but most of these men had investments in some form of Indian stores or businesses in Gravesindia and controlled the economy.

Two political parties emerged in Gravesend, each having a leader with one or more families providing core support. Joining a party was one means a person had of escaping the clutches of an exploiter. By giving allegiance to a party, an individual could depend on a large group of people to safeguard him against an extortioner. A so-called weak individual, who had few kinsmen in Gravesindia, received less support than a strong man surrounded by relatives, unless his abilities were crucial to the party. However, even a little sustenance for an émigré was better than none at all. Also, belonging to a political party or having its backing was essential in gaining leadership and political power. Thus, by providing protection to individuals, and gaining political power, the party, although present before, played a significant part in the communal life of Gravesindia.

As for the promotion of Punjabi culture, the gurdwara, as mentioned earlier, proved invaluable. The Clarence Place Sikh Temple, which the Gravesindians claim to be the largest in Great Britain, celebrated major Sikh holy days, especially birthdays of the gurus, along with some Hindu holidays like Diwali and Holi. Besakhi (a harvest festival) was the major secular holiday celebrated with an *akhand path* in the gurdwara, whereas the other Indian secular holidays came under the jurisdiction of the Indian Workers' Association and Youth Federation, which held community-wide programmes and included the English. Local talent performed along with a professional dancing or singing group. Besides Punjabi poetry, songs, and dances, there were always speeches by political and social leaders. The Indian Workers' Association[10] initially bore the main financial responsibility for these programmes, but later a collection to cover the hall expense was taken.

Party infighting had been present to some extent since the earlier years, but it became a definite part of the Punjabi lifestyle in the later period. For example, a drunken fight between members of opposite parties could lead to retaliation and counter-retaliation.[11] These conflicts were often mediated by an unbiased Gravesindian, respected by the disputants, who first consulted the elders from both families and requested them to work out a compromise. The job of mediator carried risks, and if either disputant suspected the mediator's bias, his group would eventually retaliate.

Initially, the gurdwara was the arena for party conflict, but in 1966 the locus shifted to the Indian Workers' Association. The association was formed to provide an alternative to the independent cultural broker, and it promoted Indian holidays. Unfortunately, infighting and opportunistic cultural brokers within the organization led to its demise in 1969. The local Community Relations Council (CRC) was also an arena for party conflict. One tactic used was to form 'paper organizations'; that is, one or two Punjabis declared themselves an organization like an 'Indian Cultural Society'. Since CRC membership was based on representation from organizations, one party could swell its members and influence the CRC proceedings with their influence. A few English officials in the local CRC counted these paper organizations in their statistics with pride, believing that Gravesindians were very involved in community affairs, without realizing the real purpose behind these activities.

This period also witnessed the birth of the Sikh Missionary Society in Gravesend, which later spread throughout England

7

with the purpose of proselytizing and converting the English to Sikhism and encouraging wayward Sikhs to conform. The Sikh Missionary Society published pamphlets describing Sikhism and presenting a rationale for its beliefs and practices. A language of cross-cultural communication was devised: the gurdwara was called the 'Sikh church'; Guru Nanak, the 'Sikh Saviour'; and the Granth Sahib, the 'Sikh Bible'. American converts adhering to Sikhism and its doctrine and symbols were invited to England and freely moved from gurdwara to gurdwara preaching the doctrine of the Khalsa.

Maintaining hair was, and continues to be, a major issue in the community. In the middle 1960s, a shaven Sikh was elected as gurdwara president. However, the Sikh Missionary Society tried to push through a ruling that only turbaned and bearded Sikhs were eligible for executive office in the gurdwara. But so far they have been unsuccessful because too many Gravesindian elders had had to shave their hair to acquire jobs in the early years. The Akhand Kirtan Jatha, an ultra-conservative Sikh sect, also became active at this time. This small group (about thirty members in Gravesend) not only believed in maintaining the five Sikh symbols, but also emphasized the concepts of purity and meditation. In Gravesend, nine men re-dedicated themselves to Sikhism, grew their hair, and started to uphold the Sikh symbols among their respective families.

The economy of Gravesindia and its families also changed. Indian financial advisers became part of the community, advising Punjabi immigrants on investments which would bring the best returns. This included using the stock market. Punjabis in England were beginning to invest their money in areas other than the local bank and the village. Nonetheless, money continued to flow back to the village, since England was becoming an insecure place for the Gravesindians and they wanted to ensure adequate security for themselves at home.

Simultaneously, new interests among Punjabi males between the ages of 16 and 25 emerged. They were eager to gain technical knowledge for self-enhancement—photography, electrical skills, communication technology, and telecommunication systems were but a few. Initially, only two Gravesindian boys went to college for a higher liberal arts education; the rest of the young men either worked in factories as soon as they were able or attended local technical schools to learn basic skills. Education, not the factory, later became the goal for Punjabi youth who had grown up in England.

Gravesindians also looked for work niches that gave them greater independence from an English employer. Several began peddling. After having worked their time in the factory and saving enough to purchase a business, they sold cloth, groceries, and other items, generally catering to the Punjabi community. Two Punjabis acquired Drivers' Education Schools where, for a fee, they taught driving to both English and Indians. Others sold cars, homes, accident or life insurance. Women also worked, some sewing for London retailers who stopped by the house weekly to collect the work and leave more, and others picked vegetables on the local farms, a task degrading to a Jat wife in Jandiali, but acceptable in England. Some people, both men and women, were known to hold three jobs simultaneously. In general, the Gravesindians continued to be obsessed with making money.

Although still maintaining that they planned to return to Punjab, Gravesindians began decorating their homes with wallpaper, carpeting, and furniture. They developed a sense of pride in their homes that had not been there in the early or middle years. Gardens with flowers, however, were still considered a waste of time by the Punjabis, who preferred to grow vegetables, herbs, and spices necessary to ease the food bill. Their backyards resembled miniature Punjabi fields with irrigation ditches and dirt dikes instead of waterhoses. Bathrooms and toilets were remodelled in the western style, something unheard of previously. This remodelling fostered, or was fostered by, the realization that a return to Punjab was not a possibility in the very near future, and that, in fact, there might be an extended stay in England.

Arranged marriages had also taken on a different form. In the early and middle years, the bride and groom often were from different areas; that is, if the boy lived in England, the girl usually came from Punjab, and vice versa. Rather than a girl from England, families generally preferred an uneducated village girl, who was more likely to be humble and obedient towards her mother-in-law. Young men in Punjab were happy to marry the girls abroad because it gave them an opportunity to migrate.

The 1968 immigration legislation in Britain prohibited girls in England from sponsoring boys from Punjab, but there was no ruling against boys bringing village girls. The young Punjabi émigré had to sign a letter of intent to marry a girl from Punjab. This resulted in a sad situation in Gravesindia. Because of parental choice, marriages for boys were arranged with girls from Punjab, and the Punjabi girls raised in England suffered as a result, unless their parents could afford a healthy dowry (the equivalent of a house, car, and furniture).[12] For a village girl, the dowry was comparatively meagre; it usually only included her passage and, perhaps, £200, if she had prosperous relatives in England. When the 1970 immigration legislation was being debated, the Punjabis voiced their concern about the problem to the local Member of Parliament, but it took quite a long time for the law to be changed.

English as a negative reference group

During these latter years, the Gravesindians sensed the resentment of the English towards them. The migrants had continued to view the opportunities in England as providing plenty for all. By this time, the English host community of Gravesend viewed the immigrants as contributing to the decline in the economic situation. They blamed the immigrants for overtaxing available housing and the National Health Service. 'We have worked hard to establish a good health service; now these woggies are overcrowding the services without paying sufficient taxes to support it', was a typical comment of the English. As mentioned earlier, despite claims that 'the wogs were taking positions away from us English', immigrants did not generally take away jobs the British wanted; they worked at those the English did not want because it was either shift work or a weekend job. But in Gravesend, thanks to rising unemployment, it seemed to the hosts that Punjabis were receiving preferential consideration by employers. Moreover, there were some Asians who did have excellent positions, due to their seniority in a particular company or better skills in a particular job.

One can understand the resentment of the middle- and lower-class English toward Punjabis who drove cars and paid cash for houses. It was beyond their understanding that these immigrants could acquire wealth in such a short time. The average Englishman failed to realize that, whereas he was struggling alone to make ends meet, his Punjabi colleagues were pooling their family resources. The English could not fathom how many Punjabis worked on weekends to earn 'time and a half'.

The Jats generally had more children than the English.[13] This, plus their distinctive dress and mannerisms, made them more conspicuous in the hospitals and doctors' waiting rooms. They gave the impression that they were 'reaping more benefits from the National Health Service', when actually they were not. Also, since Punjabis were unfamiliar with modern medicines, they often administered them improperly; thus, their children were frequent visitors to the emergency room and the hospital, thereby fostering an illusion of greater numbers and furthering British resentment.

Along with other immigrants, Gravesindians faced insecurity in Britain. This had been heightened by Enoch Powell and other legislators, whose advocacy of racially discriminatory practices was carried in the local and national papers. One Jat remarked, 'All Parliament has to do is pass a law and we will have to go.' Greater efforts were made to purchase land in Punjab; and land which eventually would be unavailable at any price. In the village of Jandiali, homes with extra rooms were built for the migrant brother and his family who were expected soon. But Gravesindians would not leave England voluntarily because of economic and social assets.

The British and the Punjabis, although living in proximity to each other, had radically different perspectives. However, in spite of the social barriers, it was impossible for the immigrants to remain isolated. As the negative reactions of the British to the immigrants became more sharply focused, the immigrant's behaviour underwent change.

For most Gravesindians, the British had become antagonists who attempted to block their search for success. However, there were some like the Gravesindian who said, 'I didn't even know there was discrimination until I read it in the *Observer*.' Perhaps because most discriminatory practices were remote, open hostility or resentment towards the British by the Gravesindians was minimized.[14] There was disappointment, but not hatred.

Perhaps most of them continued to consider conditions in England, with all the discrimination, better than in the village.

Punjabis did not desire to be 'black' British. They taught their children to disapprove of English mores, re-emphasized maintaining Punjabi etiquette and the five Sikh symbols. Holy men from Punjab were invited to tour gurdwaras in England and to preach Sikh doctrines. In other words, the village as the group of imitation and evaluation had become stronger. Gravesindians had become more conservative and maintained the 1950s village style of dress despite the fact that their counterparts in Punjab were wearing contemporary fashions. They preferred living in their own clusters to English neighbourhoods. To be acceptable to their reference group in Punjab, beards and hair were grown, and turbans were dug out of wardrobes by Punjabis going home on holidays. Sikhs were beginning to pressure local officials to teach Punjabi as a second language in schools instead of Latin or other European languages.

Emigration effects on Jandiali

In the home village of Jandiali, also, emigration has had its effects. The casual visitor to Jandiali now sees new multi-storey farm houses outside the village that are estimated to be worth about Rs 90,000.[15] The dates inscribed on these elaborate structures range from 1961 to 1965, indicating that they were built with money from England after the 1960 emigration boom. A few England-returnees on holiday are noticeable around the village by their elaborate dress and slipping in of English words into the stream of Punjabi conversation. But more specifically, sending members to England has affected residence patterns, social relations, village economy, and attitudes toward the British.

Concerning residence patterns, families and caste groups in Jandiali have historically formed separate blocks of settlements within the village. This situation changed when money from abroad enabled families to build larger homes, called bungalows, on the outskirts of the village. Architecturally, these homes are modernized to accommodate visiting and returning migrants. Some even boast flush toilets and ceiling fans. Every Jat migrant, whether or not he ever returns permanently to his home village, dreams of settling down in a new house on his own farm, where his next of kin will enjoy such luxuries as an indoor bath or a modern toilet.

Socially, emigration has enabled some individuals and families to acquire a standing or prestige that would not have been available previously. Jarnail Singh's narrative well illustrates the point. He came from a very poor family. His father had only two acres of land, to be divided between him and his three brothers. Partly because of their meagre financial condition, his family did not have social prestige in Jandiali. After going to England, however, Jarnail not only sent money to his family in Jandiali, but he organized collections from Jandialians abroad to help build the village school and a new gurdwara. Largely because of his efforts, the number of public buildings and roads in Jandiali has increased considerably and their quality has greatly improved. The villagers have a very high regard for Jarnail, who helped finance a bus service that has given his village-mates jobs. He has helped collect money for a school, which has given Jandiali children a good education, and he has provided a place for Jandiali emigrants to stay in in England until they are settled. Jarnail Singh and his family are now highly respected in Jandiali, and he has a strong say in local village affairs, even though he is in England.

Emigration can create a dichotomy which gives the family an opportunity to enhance its prestige or place it under censure because of the immigrant's behaviour. The émigré may have picked up English and urban ways that are considered immoral and not in accordance with village standards. And, even though a son may have a job in England which brings in money, he may come under censure because his job is polluting, such as janitorial work or cleaning latrines; or because he may not be loyal to his wife; or he may go around with western girls. Kewal Singh's case shows this, for he was a good boy who left Jandiali to make his fortune in England. He sent money home to his parents and seemed to be considerate. Kewal's father wanted to arrange a marriage for him. The bride's family, however, investigated Kewal's behaviour in England and learned that he was often drunk, slept with English girls, and had become what they considered an irresponsible person. Kewal's parents were saddened, for the marriage was not agreed upon by the bride's family and their prestige in the village was demeaned. Their son had been good to them, but he had also acquired the bad characteristics of English behaviour so that he did not have the respect he once commanded.

Going abroad does not automatically give prestige to a person or kin group. People in the village begin to lose their idealized perception of England and Punjabis in England. The emigrant from Jandiali comes under scrutiny and is evaluated according to his behaviour in England as well as his loyalty to those in Jandiali. Whereas initially he may have been free of village social controls they are now being applied to him very strictly, for the Jandialian abroad has to prove to his counterparts in Punjab that he has not been corrupted by British culture. There is, however, a certain flexibility in the case of boys, but not for girls. Immigrant Punjabi girls raised abroad are suspected of not only becoming bold and dominant, but of having lost their dignity and purity. A girl from England is considered by both the villagers in India and England to be like English girls. However, even though preference is given to a good girl straight from the village, Jandiali families seek out marriageable girls in England because they open the door to England.

Of course, having migrants in England brought changes for the village of Jandiali and other parts of Punjab. Without emigration, Jandiali and some other parts of Punjab might have been the scene of starvation and poverty instead of being prosperous and devoloped as they are today. No one knows how much money comes back to Punjab from abroad—until the government liberalized the foreign exchange regulations, the money used to enter through the black market. In 1971 the villages enjoyed the black market exchange rate of Rs 36 to the pound, and were unaware of the official rate of around Rs 18 to the pound. One black market agent at that time claimed that a million pounds a day went from Great Britain to India; however, this seemed to me to be an exaggerated figure. It was also alleged by black market agents in 1971 that, owing to the ingenuity of the English, no gold left England. They claimed that English companies in India, by the Indian government's decree, had to reinvest a percentage of their profits in India.

According to these Punjabis, since all English profits could not leave India, immigrants in England gave their earnings in England to companies, and the branch in India paid the designated villager, thus transferring profits to England and migrant money to India.

During this period, the Indian government allowed Punjabis abroad to send gifts to their relatives in the homeland. The Massey Ferguson Tractor Company in England arranged for Punjabis in England to buy tractors with one-year guarantees and delivered them to Punjab. An Indian representative taught the villagers how to use the tractor. Between 24 October 1968 and 31 August 1970, 1,038 Massey Ferguson tractors that were delivered in Punjab were paid for in sterling by Indian residents in England. The cost per tractor was about Rs 21,000, and in the village of Jandiali six of the eight tractors were purchased with English money.

In 1971, a rough estimate of visible assets, such as houses and tractors, which were provided by money from abroad, was about one million rupees, although the actual investment from England may be close to three times that amount.

Jandiali has benefited not only from money, but also from innovative ideas, new farming methods, and new business techniques from abroad. England-returnee Jats often write to friends in the United States, England, and Europe for farm journals and new seed varieties. Jandialians on holiday from England, Canada, or the United States teach villagers the latest farming techniques.

An overview of cities like Phagwara, Goraya, and Jullundur, with their rapid economic growth in the past ten years, shows the effect of money from abroad on the landscape. The thirty-mile road between Ludhiana and Jullundur is studded with small businesses, car part works, tool shops, iron and steel works, to name just a few, which have mushroomed within the last decade with money from abroad.

The following example of a family with one brother in the village and four brothers and two married sisters with their respective families in Gravesend illustrates the impact of money earned abroad. The brother in the village runs an iron works factory with his two sons and farms the family's forty acres in the village. He divides his time and energy between the farm, factory, and house, riding a Honda motorcycle and claiming no desire to migrate because he has all he needs and more in Punjab, including a pukka house with ceiling fans. In his homeland he says, 'I am the master, so why should I go and slave as a labourer like my brothers in English factories?' Obviously, he has not become prosperous just from farming, but is greatly assisted by the money that has flowed in from England. Money, innovative ideas, and diminished pressure on existing resources by emigration give advantages to Jandiali and other Doaba villages.

Jandiali emigration has been good for the village in general. Emigrants in Gravesend and Leamington Spa have provided the capital for paving roads, building two school houses, constructing two wedding houses, and collecting enough money for a new gurdwara. Besides, the Cooperative Bank continually has a surplus of cash, which is unusual for a village the size of Jandiali.[16]

With wealth, however, has come inflation. The price of an acre of land in Jandiali has soared from Rs 4,000 in 1954 to Rs 12,000 in 1968, to Rs 25,000 in 1971, to Rs 30,000 in 1978. The villagers maintain that there is no land for sale at any price, and during this study, no land transactions were observed.

True to their character, Jandialians from both Punjab and England buy land with their wealth. Land is considered a safe buy and is preferred as a form of investment. Since it has become impossible to buy land in Jandiali, they are purchasing land in neighbouring Punjabi states, Rajasthan and Uttar Pradesh. Kessinger (1974:155) observed similar behaviour.

Not all village members benefit from emigration. Inflation and increased dowries take their toll on those who do not have assets from abroad. They find it difficult to survive, for they can neither buy land nor improve their situation. True, there are more jobs for some, and schooling is readily available for their children; but these things do not necessarily improve their lot.

For both the Jandialians in England and in the home village, their perception of the British has changed. The British are perceived as blocking the advancement of their brothers, and being an England-returnee is losing the prestige it once had. The Jandialians in Punjab see the landless emigrants as inferior Jats who take orders instead of being their own masters of the land. Villagers are aware of the immoral behaviour of the English, and they assume that Sikhs in England are readily corrupted by it. Also, villages stereotype the emigrants in the same manner they do westerners; that is, rich but unable to stand the rigours of village life. Gravesindians either do not realize that change in the attitude of the villagers, or are unwilling to admit it. They continue to come home as England-returnees and show off their status. Outwardly, the villagers treat them royally because of their wealth; but privately, Jandialians comment on the sojourners' inferior status as landless Sikh Jats.

The situation in England is watched very closely by the Indian press. Its coverage, for example, of the strike by Sikh transportation workers in Wolverhampton (Beethan 1970) aroused sympathetic demonstrations in India.[17] Such articles incite anger and remorse among the Indians, especially the relatives of migrants. The Jandialians, along with the rest of India, have become more aware of British discrimination, and esteem for the British has dropped. However, some Jandiali elders and urban Punjabis continue to glorify the English and blame the migrant's problems on his own immaturity.

The aftermath of the 1962 legislation has contributed to the establishment of Gravesindia as a permanent Sikh Jat community in England, although the Punjabis themselves are not willing to admit it. The immigrants in Gravesend continue to deal with family tensions, exploiters, and the problems of their children. Now they have to face the future of their children, who are British by birth. The following chapter sets forth their perspectives in their own words.

CHAPTER VII

FACING THE FUTURE

To stay or not

The last three chapters have shown that the situation of the Jandiali–Gravesend migrants changed over the years. Emigration, which had originally been a temporary phenomenon, took on a permanence. The Gravesindians have stayed in England longer than they had expected. Thus in 1970, the migrant faced the question of whether or not to stay on in England. Many had been in England over fifteen years and had, according to Punjab standards, made their fortune. Others had returned to Punjab only to lose their fortunes, and were compelled to return to England. The obvious problem for most immigrants was whether to become English or maintain separatism with all of its undesirable repercussions of discrimination and ostracism from British society. The Punjabi immigrant wanted the best of both worlds, and he was torn by conflicting values. As one Sikh Jat said, 'We have one foot in England and the other in India, and it hurts in the middle.'

This chapter examines these conflicts as articulated during a community debate. It must be kept in mind that people do not necessarily adhere to the principles that they advocate in such a meeting; but the reader will gain an insight into the problems and solutions that the Gravesindians considered. The illustrative example centres on the Gravesindians' debate over opening a Khalsa (Sikh community) school. The debate was held on a holiday to enable all interested parties to attend and actively participate, and reveals a wide spectrum of community attitudes.

The debate: 'We need a Khalsa school'

Concern over the founding of a Khalsa school stemmed from the formation of the Sikh Missionary Society (hereafter SMS), which was founded in Gravesend. As described earlier, this group of concerned Sikhs published pamphlets and sought to defend and propagate Sikhism in England. When two of their members' children were refused admission into an English public school on the basis of thinly disguised discrimination, the core group of the SMS decided that it was time to found a Khalsa public school. Gurdwaras all over England were informed about the idea and their co-operation solicited. In the meantime, the core group started seeking support from the Gravesindian community at large. Finally, a date was fixed for a public meeting in the gurdwara to discuss the issues. Patrons of Sikhism, Punjabi school teachers, and interested educated people were officially notified. Punjabi representatives came from Dartford, Gillingham, and other parts of Kent. Upon arrival at the Clarence Place Gurdwara, everyone went to the basement for some Punjabi tea, rich with milk and sugar. The Sikhs in England say that they always eat or have tea together before a meeting, for Guru Gobind Singh taught that people who eat together do not fight.

The cold, damp basement came alive as the forty-two people attending stood around in groups drinking hot tea, talking and laughing.[1] Some joked and gossiped, while others disseminated their views on the pending issue. It became clear that the group was sharply divided. There were heated discussions between the shaven and non-shaven Sikhs over a recently published pamphlet written by Kirpal Singh (1971:15) which stated that the Sikh who cuts his hair is a cheat! There was a rumour about a disagreement between the SMS and the Gurdwara Committee concerning who should run the proposed school, how it should be operated, and what its purpose should be. However, none of these discussions surfaced in the meeting, which started late.[2]

Key passages from the Granth Sahib were read, and the meeting began with a welcome from the Secretary of the gurdwara, Makhan Singh, who then introduced the President of the gurdwara, Roshan Singh, a tall, impressive Sikh from Jandiali who greeted the gathering and made a few brief remarks:

As President of the gurdwara committee, I welcome you to our gurdwara and am happy you honoured our invitation by coming. We are in dire need of a school. Our brothers who teach in the schools are best qualified to talk on this subject, for we only work in factories and read newspapers; hence we know little. They will tell us why we need a Khalsa school, how money can be collected and affiliation obtained.

He then turned the microphone over to Mr Sondhi, a school teacher in the Gravesend school system, one of the leaders of the SMS and a promoter of the school.

Everyone has the right to differing opinions, and each individual speaks for himself, not for the society or organization he belongs to. I would like to explain the education system in Gravesend to you.

After describing the English and Gravesend school system, he continued:

Unfortunately, most Indian children are sent to the secondary school where they study until the age of 16. They are neither taught with exams in view nor given a real education. The enterprising children, encouraged by parents, may work for the CSC [a secondary school certificate exam]. Since their teachers do not take interest, most of our children just bide time until they come of age and can work in a factory or some comparable job. A few, who perform outstandingly in the CSC, are put on the GCE 'O'[3] level course and have the door open to colleges.

Our children have special problems, as they came here at a late age of 8 and 10, hardly knew any English to prove their academic standing, and did not have time to learn the language. Hence, 90 per cent of our children have been judged wrongly. As a teacher, I can authoritatively say their English may be weak, but our children are better in math and science. They are 'A' level[4] material in any five subjects; if English Language was not necessary and Punjabi was included, our children would be able to go on to higher education.

My daughter was not selected for upper school. I appealed, but to no avail. Consequently, I paid to send her to the Bexley Public School. The first term she was fifth in her class of 27. Undoubtedly, the child had the ability, just as many other Indian children have.

What do we want our children to be? As parents, we desire our children to do well academically and pursue a career. And our children have only two alternatives, either do well in the 11 plus exams or go to a public school in Bexley or Chatham. Willingly we will pay for the latter. I have personally taken six children to Bexley who were examined by the headmaster for one hour each and judged acceptable. However, the headmaster recommended that the children have an English hair cut, with which we could not comply. Our personal liberty was violated, and because they were Sikhs, the boys were not admitted to the school.

Oxford and Cambridge universities have arrangements for Hindi and Punjabi. I am an examiner, but in the past four years I have not read any papers, as none of our children take the exams. Schools have no arrangements for teaching Punjabi. When our children return to India, speaking and knowing only English, they are once again faced with difficulties. Thus, Punjabi and Hindi should be taught and examined. What is the use of this big gurdwara when there is no person to become a *Granthi*, for in twenty years no one will be able to read our scriptures. Use your money to run a school for all religions and cultures, with a high standard of education, like our schools in America, Canada, and Malaya. Where the money will come from, and other details, will be discussed later.

Mr Choona, from London, a rich businessman who sells insurance and deals with investment counselling and stocks, was called. He was given pre-eminence as a tactic to get people with money behind the project. Like Mr Sondhi, he, too, was turbaned and a former school teacher. 'I agree with Sondhi's views', he said.

I know, for I have taught three years in a girls' school. The educational advisor and the secretary of education in the borough of Ealing were prejudiced against the Punjabis. They refused us advancement because of our accent, weak English Language, or what they called lack of knowledge.

There was one special case of a smart boy who was not allowed to sit for the eleven plus, I am sure because of his hair. They said, 'The boy looks incapable and unintelligent.' When a test was requested, they gave the boy a seven-minute test on which the child did poorly. 'This proves my point,' said the secretary. No wonder; three of the seven questions were on English grammar. The boy never had the opportunity to prove himself in grammar school. I am not saying all this because of prejudice. All four of my children went to grammar schools. Intelligence tests were, and still are, based on the English language and culture, which keeps our Punjabi children out.

It is very sad that our children wear crosses around their necks and do not wear the *karha*. Our children know nothing about our religion, but learn about Christianity from religious education. Our girls do not want boys with long hair. I blame the parents, who are busy working in factories and fighting political battles instead of educating their daughters in the Sikh religion as Christians are taught everything about Christianity. Our philosophy and history should counteract the

Christian religious teachings. There should be debates about Sikhism and Christianity. We cannot blame the Christians for preaching their religion, but we should teach our children about our own beliefs.

Girls are openly taught by English teachers that their parents are wrong in not giving them freedom. So far, our girls neither have boyfriends nor associate with the opposite sex. If our children do not love our culture and religion, they will not love us, their parents, and their homes. If we think about an issue after it has happened, we are not wise, but foolish. We should prevent our girls from going on the wrong road before we have to repent.

We descend from the Sikh Gurus who, five hundred years ago, went to every corner of India preaching the faith. In spite of this, we are so few and still do not teach our children our faith to expand it. We should be missionaries and tell these English about our religion, for we are fortunate to be born Sikhs.

I am happy that in Gravesend the people and the Sikh Missionary Society have preached Sikhism, and their goal is, by the grace of Guru Nanak, to widen the scope of Sikhism.

Both these men had talked very long, so discussion followed as to whether a time limit should be given to each speaker. It was decided by consensus that each speaker would be allowed only five minutes, although this rule was hardly adhered to.

The next speaker was Sardar Jarman Singh, a big, burly Punjabi ex-policeman and a national volley ball player in India.

Sports people from all over the world asked me about my religion and culture. We feel that our symbols are a stumbling block to our religion, but actually they glorify us. In India, there are lots of Christian and Hindu schools and colleges. My own sister studies in a Sanatan Dharam school in Jullundur, and she learns about the Hindu religion; but she is a Sikh. The headmaster of the Khalsa school would not pass anyone unless he could say the *gurbani*. Our children go to churches on Sundays to get a cap. Christians instil competition which is good. I was the only Sikh on the Olympic volley ball team, and I was recognized everywhere because of my Sikhism. It was very beneficial, and I agree with everything the two Singhs have said previously.

Our children are called 'dirty' or asked questions like 'Why do you look like this?' If our children know about the symbols, they will not have an inferiority complex, but will be proud of their distinctiveness. Unfortunately, we do not know anything about our national symbols or our anthem. To create a national spirit, our children should be educated. *Goras*[5] are really no better, because most of them do not know their national symbols either.

If we are worried about our children, we should do what Professor Khwaja, a Cambridge University mathematics professor, did. In the pre-partition days, he saw his daughter on an Englishman's arm. When she introduced her boy-friend to him, he did not say anything, but immediately decided to return to India, and became the principal of Islamia College, Lahore. He did this to take his daughter home to her own culture. Yes, a school is necessary for national and cultural enhancement.

Mr Ujjal Singh, a shaven Sikh and a school teacher in the local English school system, spoke:

Our children are not the only ones who suffer; English children suffer also. Even if we do have our own Khalsa public school, our children will have to sit for the same standardized exams and maintain a standard. The child who is willing to learn will learn under any circumstances. It is also the desire of Sikh parents to enhance Gurmukhi.

Concerning religion, when I take assembly, with the headmaster's permission, I tell all kinds of Indian stories, the life of Gandhi and other leaders and gurus, and stories from the Granth Sahib. Educators agree that children should have a comprehensive religious education in all religions. If Sondhi and Choona have experienced only Christian preaching in the schools, then my five years' experience in an all-white school, with no immigrant children whatsoever, has been different from theirs.

There should be an organization which teaches our religion without its superstitions, and the richness of our culture without our caste differences. Such classes should be held on weekends in the gurdwara. There is no need to open a Khalsa school, because we will just get further away and more separated from the English.

Immediately following was Sardar Kuldip Singh, a stout, turbaned Sikh, formerly from Malaysia, now from the Greater London area.

Everyone has differing views; hence, one should not say nasty things about another religion, as God is the centre, and everyone has to go to him eventually. Sikhism will not end with its young history and rich culture. Sikhs have been in Malaysia since the seventeenth century, and there are many Khalsa schools which instil the necessity of beards and hair. Two of our boys with uncut hair went for higher education to Australia. The headmaster of their school invited them to his house to learn about Sikhism, but the boys knew nothing about the symbols. However, they were intelligent enough to write home immediately for information. Gyani Mohan Singh sent a letter giving details and

8

reasons why Sikhs have long hair and maintain other symbols; this information the boys gave the headmaster. Eager to know about their religion, they asked their parents for books. This incident led to the establishment of the Guru Nanak Institute in Malaysia, not just for general education, but to teach Sikhism. Schools should be for everyone, not just Sikh children. Sikhism should be taught with adaptation to the host country, without compromising the culture of our blood country.

Another problem we faced in Malaysia was our girls falling in love with Chinese boys. Although mothers explained it was wrong to go out with boys, they could not get the point across. Our girls failed to understand why it was wrong to do what other girls did. Our missionaries, and gurdwaras should aim toward teaching our religion. When we bring our young to the gurdwara for worship, we should come ourselves. A gurdwara is not for factionalism, but for spreading love and learning the *gurbani*. No child can become an engineer by learning from his father. Similarly, our children cannot become religious sitting at home. Our Khalsa education board should be formed to get educational rights and affiliation.

The former secretary of the Gravesend gurdwara, Mr Sarjan, was called. Like Ujjal, he was shaven. He had been a science teacher at the Pelham Road Grammar School for four years, and had taught in India for five years prior to his migration. He said,

My experience might help. I was invited to a Christian meeting where I shared my Sikh religion. I was asked if I was planning on staying in England, and I answered affirmatively, to which one of them said, 'It is difficult for a coloured person to stay in a white country'. This portrays the feelings of these *goras* toward us. They are curious about us, but have no intention to convert us. Two Sikh girls in my grammar school wanted to become Christians, but I talked them out of it. Christian conversion is not the aim of the British, but they make religious education very appealing to our females. If we want to protect our girls from Christianity, we have to make our faith very attractive to them.

English grammar schools have the top 16 per cent of the intelligent students, but there are a negligible number of Punjabi children who get in. I know of students as intelligent as those I teach who were not recommended for grammar school.

The system of education in England is different,[6] hence our children who did well in India will not necessarily do well here; not because they are any less intelligent, but because they are not familiar with this system and the English language. From this meeting, I gather Punjabis feel public schools are the answer, but they are expensive, and few parents can afford them for each child. We should take effective steps for future improvements in the present education system so it will benefit the common man.

Ranjit Singh had been in England fifteen years. A husky, shaven Sikh who had been teaching in the English school system, he informed the audience in brief, but no uncertain terms, that the idea of a Khalsa public school was a segregationalist one. He had been a Khalsa school drop-out in India:

Religion and education cannot be separated and yet should be. India has more Christians than Sikhs, for the former spend money on their missionaries, who preach the religion and bring in converts. As far as Sikh religious education is concerned, we parents should certainly teach and preach our religion to swell our numbers, but concerning the school, it is too big and expensive a project. Racial harmony is obtained by mixing, not by isolating. How many other kinds of coloured children and white children will come to our Khalsa school? A Khalsa school will create problems of integration just like those schools in the United States. Separate schools will have different standards of education. If vocational education is important and needed for our children, then it should be taught on weekends and holidays. The greatest danger of segregated schools is that they will create social problems.

With that, he gave the floor to Sardar Gurmeet Singh, M.A., a bearded Sikh, and author who wrote a pamphlet on the Sikh Symbols, a publication of the SMS.

Our children in England are our prime concern. We want to maintain our culture and religion, and although I realize that there is a danger, we can overcome it by following the teachings of our gurus. A Khalsa school will be advantageous to Sikhism for it will emphasize an international need and the oneness of humanity in spite of cultural diversities. Religion is of prime importance, whether it is Christianity, Islam, Hinduism, or Sikhism. Sikhism has the best qualities of all the religions and should be spread to all nations. We would produce individuals from our school who are so strong in their faith that they can pray in gurdwaras, mosques, or churches. If we produce narrow-minded children, then our project will go unfulfilled. We come from a different culture, which does not make it a lesser culture. Hence, it is our duty to remove the inferiority complex from the minds of our children who, because they cannot speak good English, are considered 'non-intellectuals'. Any child who wants to do well should be given the opportunity.

The Tory government has been in power for many years and believes in class separatism. The Teachers' Union wanted comprehensive education, which the Tories refused. Our school will be for children who are frustrated because of their colour and turbans. The aim should be to place children on a par with grammar school children. Our children have had a weak education because of the lack of furniture, books, and libraries in our Punjabi schools. But the school here should glorify Guru Nanak and be an example of maintaining a very high standard.

There are two kinds of schools, vocational and academic. The former is for those children who are not considered grammar school material, whereas the latter is to educate the intelligent student to pass GCE exams and go to college. One school is not enough, but honesty, religion, and both cultures should be taught, keeping in view that some things about English culture are good and should be accepted, but reject those which are incompatible with our Hindu heritage. We should instil pride in our religion and culture. The aim of education is to give identity and pride in one's heritage. The British education system is narrow and only concentrates on teaching students to fit in a Christian world, not a universal world. Our school should have the wider scope of a universal world. . . . What is the use of a gurdwara if we cannot train our children in Sikhism?

The discussion which followed concentrated on the discontent of Sikh girls being forced to marry their parents' choice of husband. It was moved and seconded that this was a cultural matter and had nothing to do with the school. The lunch break followed; those who favoured the school sat together during the meal, whereas those who were opposed and neutral sat at a different table.

When the meeting resumed, Surjit, the President of the Indian Youth Federation, was the next to speak. He had come to England at the age of 13, straight from the village, and learned English after his arrival in England. Now, at nineteen, he was in college.

I want to congratulate those who thought of this scheme. There are twenty[7] Punjabi college students in Gravesend, so I will share with you how we feel with regard to a Khalsa school. There are three reasons given for opening this school: to pass the eleven plus exams, to expound Sikhism, and to control our children. We all know that the first reason is irrelevant because the eleven plus exams will be abolished when the Labour Party comes in. Where the second is concerned, I am a believer that Sikhism must be taught to our children and maintained, but it is not a sufficient reason to open a school. Sikhism can be taught in our gurdwara Sunday School, by educating parents, and by evening classes. It is not necessary to waste money on a public school, for our people cannot really afford such a venture; besides, such a school would be predominantly for immigrants and would create an unhealthy social separation.

We Indians who go to college do not speak fluent English, are socially inept, and still fight among ourselves. At college we have to compete with the *goras*, but we have two disadvantages, colour and language. Colour we cannot change, but we can improve our language to be on par with the white man whom we compete with. We should know them well, and this can only be done by mingling with them, not by being apart.

Our people work in factories, drink beer, and associate only with Indians. They do not learn to socialize with the English for fear their children will get out of control and emulate British ways. Our children must be given freedom so they can become one with the world. Our Guru Gobind Singh would have said all whites, Chinese, and Africans are one. Sikhism teaches oneness.

Next, Mr P. Singh came to the podium. A local teacher and shaven Sikh, he later became a member of the gurdwara committee.

Our religion is necessary, our culture is necessary, and our education is necessary. Undoubtedly, all three are a responsibility of the parents. But we limit ourselves and become narrow-minded in our venture if we call this a Khalsa school. Our Indian children will neither fit in English society nor be able to cope with the vast competition if we open a school of our own standards.

We should only take steps on an experimental basis, like getting into the academic councils and eliminating discrimination. If our children are sent to India for education[8] or we open a public school, we create a division among ourselves—between those who are rich and can afford either, and those who cannot afford it. The latter's children will become factory workers, and only rich children will avail themselves of the opportunity. If we take a wrong step, our future generation will not be able to rectify it easily. This set-up which is being proposed will not provide a Sikh cultural education for the whole immigrant community.

After each speaker, the audience discussed the arguments of

the speaker. Bibi Prakash Kaur, the wife of the Malaysian who spoke earlier and a teacher for twelve years, was called upon for her views.

We talk about missionary schools and how they preach; we must remember that Christian missionaries have strong backgrounds, and we do not. We tend to complain about the financial burden of our children's education. My fifteen-year-old daughter's education has only cost us £60 in the past three years. She speaks perfect English and is an outstanding student because she wanted to become a doctor, and I took an interest in her academics. But now, at fifteen, they have stopped her higher education and shattered her hopes. The education board does not think she has the academic credentials for medical college, but we think so and are appealing her case. Educational training is very important. Religious education should be given on holidays and weekends in various gurdwaras with the support of the Sikh Missionary Society. The result of the Guru Nanak Institute in Malaya was a complete success, and we did not hear complaints of the cost. If a parent does not want to spend money on a child's education, whom does he earn for? This school in Gravesend should provide an international education.

Amrit Singh, the secretary of the SMS, then spoke.

This school will be such that every child can get an education. English public schools are for a few and are very expensive. They are a white elephant and only help a few rich children without being an educational guarantee. Instead, a comprehensive school will be much more beneficial to our needs. The Tories want 60 per cent of the people uneducated . . . 'Squelch labour' is their motto, but we must make some kind of school which will be beneficial for everyone, not for just a few élite. We must get a grant for our school even though the Tories favour anti-comprehensive education. We are not opening a school just to show people that we have a Khalsa school in England. Our goal is to have a school with a high standard just as the *goras* schools, regardless of our insecure position here due to the forthcoming Immigration bill.[9]

Many points had been raised, so Sondhi set forth propositions concerning the financing and philosophy of the proposed school. Then he continued:

You have to make arrangements for all subjects according to needs. Not all children from our school will be sent for higher education. But our system promises to be very tough, with difficult assignments and homework.[10]

Concerning the cultural issue: When I see our children with their fashionable hair styles, lipstick, bare legs, some even with cigarettes, going to school dances, and secretly meeting boys, I am made aware that this is the effect of English culture. If you sit too close to the fire, you will get burned, and that is exactly what is happening to the next generation. Concerning religion, it is the most vital part of our Punjabi culture and heritage, and certainly will be taught by competent teachers. Undoubtedly, such a school will be expensive and cater to the rich, but we have not decided what the fees will be. If all the gurdwaras are generous with their contributions and keep them up, it may even be free, or have a nominal tuition fee. In India, a public school costs Rs 300 a month, and in England they cost £38 a term. If I can afford to send one child to a public school and Ujjal can send two, why is it not possible for our factory friends, who make more money than us school teachers, to pay for the education of their children?

Prem, one of the Indian Youth Federation leaders, interrupted. 'How many people think like you?' Sondhi replied, 'If we can look after our animals well, why not our children?' One old man spoke, 'We are too few here to make the decision for such a school. How much money is needed anyway?' Sondhi ignored his comment and continued, 'I believe in freedom, but not early in life, because one fault is always unforgivable, that is freedom of girls.'

Then Bibi Usha, a Punjabi visitor in the community with an M.A. from the United States, decided it was time somebody defended the Punjabi girls.

I do not know if I have the right to speak at this meeting, but listening to the speeches today I am very much saddened. The impression given us is that this school is for your sons, and yet you all complain about the girls with bare legs, smoking, using lipstick, with crosses around their necks, knowing more about Christianity than Sikhism. If you want to teach Sikhism to your children, you must start teaching at home, from childhood. Our adults know very little of their own religious and cultural heritage. Besides, they are more theoretical than practical, which confuses the children and makes them wonder. We must instil trust in our children and give them freedom. The family and what is learned in the family is of utmost importance. From my own experience, I went to a convent school in India and lived in the boarding house for nine months of each year. I always stood first in religious education, but that did not convert me to Catholicism; my family heritage was too strong. From babyhood, we heard stories of our religious and national leaders. Also, my father allowed me to go with my legs bare until I was fourteen, when it was time to switch to salwar-kameez. To this day, I prefer my national dress and proudly wear it even in America. All of you firmly believe that Punjabi women must keep their native dress, and yet look at yourselves, all in western suits. You put girls in their native dress at the age of five, and then they rebel when they get the chance.

If you want your children to keep the religion, you must educate yourselves first and also get some competent teachers of religious education in the gurdwara. My father, a prominent doctor, was educated in England and the United States, and yet returned to India to settle down. You want to settle here in England, make good money, but not even learn the English language. Some of our Punjabi brothers have been here for over twenty years and still do not speak any English. However, we are not slow to complain about the British and their immigration laws, and we fear being turned out of this country. What is the point of schools for the children when the parents cannot even adapt here? Do not be too critical of your daughters; every Punjabi girl is conscious of the izzat of her family.

Harnam Singh, who claims to have walked closely with Gandhi and considers himself a revolutionary, spoke:

I was not intending to participate in today's discussion, but listening to Bibi Usha made me want to speak. I agree with everything she has said. Our history is very rich, but like the Brahmins, we believe in theory, not in practice. Education is not sixteen classes, for Ranjit Singh had only studied one class and was the best administrator. Strength is of great importance, but we should not be narrow-minded. We should learn from the good things of others; instead we have learned from the *goras* only to go to pubs and drink. Drunkenness is bad, and I suggest that a £5 fine should be imposed on anyone smelling of alcohol coming near the gurdwara. Christian missionaries —look what they have done for our country, its education system, its hospitals and charities. We cannot compete with them, but fear that they will convert us.

After a brief, but humorous dialogue with the audience, Harnam Singh continued,

We have 56 gurdwaras in England and still need another institution for our religious enhancement? Religious foundations should be laid by the parents; children should be trained at home. The gurdwara should offer courses in Gurmukhi, and it is the duty of parents to make use of gurdwara facilities. We must unite as a community. What can we teach our young when the shaven Sikh ridicules his bearded brother in front of the *goras*? Like the churches, the gurdwara should take religious education upon itself. Later, when there is a lucrative source of income, think of a school.

Speeches that followed reiterated what had been said previously. Jasjit Singh of Chatham, one of the last speakers before open discussion, said,

The education system of every nation keeps its own needs prime. My main points of concern are three. Can the product of the Khalsa school be accepted to fit in English society? Our appearance keeps us out of public schools. Will our appearance open English society to us because we went to a Khalsa school? Will our Khalsa school and educated children be successful in this society with all its demands? If the answer to these points is in the affirmative, then this school is necessary; otherwise not.

Next, the secretary of the gurdwara took the podium. Although his son, a turbaned lad of thirteen, had been beaten up several times on the way home from school by some white gangs, and once was whipped with a belt by a bigger white boy, he said,

Our children will become isolated from English society, and I agree with Bibi Usha that we should not separate ourselves from our host country. I do believe, however, that vocational education is important.

Debate between supporters and opponents followed. Finally, Roshan Singh, the gurdwara President, took the microphone.

After listening to various people and their points of view, we are aware that there is a problem; discrimination exists, and we need a school. But, we have to consider seriously what kind of school we want, because we do not wish to become isolated from the English. The good examples of Kenyan and Malaysian schools should be followed, upholding high standards of learning. If we had our own school, those children who would have been unable to get an education will benefit.

Let us not quibble over petty differences; they will solve themselves once the major question is resolved. Our Punjabi teachers will take pains to impart education and raise our standards. There is a definite need for a school; hence, we must have another meeting, with better representation, for more points of view.

Roshan Singh then tried in vain to direct a general discussion. Instead, bedlam broke loose, and the meeting became quite disorderly. The few concrete comments were, 'We should vote to see if another meeting is necessary'. 'There are too few people here to make a decision.' 'We have sacrificed five hours.' Sondhi stood up and shouted, 'President Sardar Balwant Singh has pledged £10,000 towards the school on behalf of the Southall Gurdwara.' He aimed to swing opinion in his favour, but few must have heard him, because everyone was shouting. Then a loud '*Bole Sonehal*'[11] echoed and was followed by the response '*Sat Sri Akal*';[12] normality was briefly resumed.

The school supporters announced from the floor that the next meeting would be held in the London area. Following the suggestion from the floor, Roshan Singh attempted to form a committee to study the matter further. The first nomination was Ujjal Singh, who refused to serve; thus, the attempt failed.

More discussion ensued. Ujjal Singh was heard to say, 'We should include the English', to which someone retorted, 'Did the English include us when they passed the Immigration bill?' Everyone tiredly walked out, talking all the while, and Roshan Singh was saying, 'I thank you all'.

Since this debate, no further developments concerning the Khalsa school have materialized. Weekend Gurmukhi classes continue at the Gravesend gurdwara, which has also received permission to open a nursery school on its premises.

Some of the participants of this study behave in a different manner than their speeches indicate. For example, Ujjal Singh advocated assimilation, yet he is very particular that his family live in the proper Punjabi manner—maintaining separateness from the host community. But Sondhi, Jarman Singh, and Surjit Singh all behave in the manner they advocated. To try to put the issues raised by this debate into perspective, it seems that the Jandiali émigré, whether he is fully aware of his decision or not, does not intend to return to Punjab. It is also true, however, that his homeland continues to be his source of security and provides the cultural norms by which his behaviour in England is evaluated. Standing between two cultures, the Gravesindians are looking for a niche for their children that will give them respectability and acceptance in the eyes of both the Punjabis and the English.

It has been shown that the Punjabi Sikh Jats are capable of making adaptive changes, but their flexibility is being challenged. No longer is it sufficient for the Gravesindians to amass a fortune (either in their own eyes or in the eyes of their Jandiali relatives). They are struggling to adopt the British cultural value of education and the kinds of careers and service positions that education makes possible. It seems that change is occurring to the extent that education is increasing in importance.

Their efforts to adjust are apparent in the concern voiced that their children—especially their sons—are being denied admission to the better public schools. It is clear, too, in their desire that their children be able to compete on a par with English students when seeking university admission or jobs.

Those in favour of the Khalsa school expressed their intention of providing a school that would prepare the younger generation to take advantage of any and all educational and vocational opportunites available to them, and for which they have the ability. The discrimination practised by the English does not allow for this, and they are concerned that the habit of maintaining purity will be threatened by their children's education in English schools. They are concerned, too, by the lack of young men interested in their religion and eager to promulgate it. According to them, the strong religious training in the Khalsa school would rectify this lack of training in religion and other cultural values. It would also safeguard their girls, the bearers of family izzat, from pollution. Female purity is thought to be jeopardized by the encouragement of their English school teachers and co-education.

While those who oppose the Khalsa school share these concerns for maintaining the purity of the girls, they feel this task is the responsibility of the family and gurdwara. A Khalsa school might accomplish this, but there is the risk of a profound loss. Such a school would further separate the Punjabis from the British, thus limiting opportunities for their young people. It would not even supply the needed skills, they suggested. Important, in fact essential, for an immigrant's full participation in British life is a comprehensive knowledge of the English language. These debaters feel that the Khalsa school could not provide this. They also fear that its faculty might not be able to keep up with the English, nor have access to new developments in academia.

It became apparent, too, that those opposed to the Khalsa

school had begun to make an additional adaptive change. It seemed that maintaining purity is no longer strong enough as a value to require separatism in education. They began to criticize what they feel were bad aspects of their culture, especially that which they have termed 'superstitious', and feel that these traits should not be fostered in their children.

The debate dealt with a behavioural problem—the means of living satisfactorily with a new goal, that of education. Separate education in a Khalsa school might provide greater opportunity at present for academic development, but it might also close doors in the future. Attending public school required compromising religious values (cutting one's hair and so forth) and left one in danger of pollution, but it kept the doors open. A Khalsa school would safeguard the cultural heritage now being lost, because parents spent so much time working that they neglected this aspect of their children's training. On the other hand, there was no guarantee that the immigrant teachers would have the skills necessary to prepare their students for competition in an English-speaking world. These were the issues of the debate, issues for which no solution could then be found.

Closer attention to the people who took part in the debate brings the issues into sharper focus. The discussions in the gurdwara basement prior to the school debate were generally among the western-educated Sikhs. This was as true of those who had long hair and beards and favoured the Khalsa school as it was for those who were shaven and opposed it. Western education seemed to pressure the Sikh into making a basic choice, either to keep his hair and uphold religion, or cut his hair and reject Sikh symbols. It was a difficult decision to make, but once it was made, the Punjabi stuck wholeheartedly to his position. Thus, those who chose the former alternative often became ultra-conservative and dogmatic in their approach to the Sikh religious system.

These two groups had two things in common. First, all the speakers (except Surjit Singh and the woman visitor from the United States) had a properly arranged marriage (by Punjabi standards). They had provided, too, for properly arranged marriages for their children. Thus, whether shaven or bearded, these immigrants clung to this aspect of traditional requirements. Second, as Bibi Usha pointed out, all the men present were in western attire. It seems that they found compromise in some aspects acceptable for themselves, but would not allow it for their women and children. Women had to wear the traditional salwar-kameez.[13] The men (and a few women) enjoyed associating with the English, but the other members of the community were forbidden to do so.

In Gravesend, these conflicts had not been resolved. Perhaps before resolving them the Gravesindians had to face the issue of their length of stay in England. The next chapter examines the various aspects of this issue and their significance.

CHAPTER VIII

WHY STAY IN ENGLAND?

The Situation

Originally, the Punjabi Sikh Jat migrants had planned to return to their homeland once their fortunes were made, but a change in British immigration laws and a shift in the migrants' attitudes has resulted in their deciding to remain. Why have they chosen to do so, and how will they combat British influence? How will Gravesindians protect their children from cultural corruption by English ways? These are some of the questions that have to be resolved in the migrant community.

The Gravesend–Jandiali migrants do not seem happy. They do not manifest the same carefree security shown by their village counterparts in Punjab. In England, they are second-class citizens, and although it is not a major concern to them, Gravesindians frequently receive rude treatment from the English. British passports, not issued in London, do not bring the same treatment for blacks as they do for whites. This was true, for instance, in the case of passports issued to Asians in Kenya. The Gravesindians read about these situations in the papers even if they do not experience similar treatment themselves. Many Punjabis patronize their own shops in order to have minimal contact with the British people because of the existing problem of discrimination.

Why do the Gravesend–Jandiali migrants continue to stay in a country where they are not wanted and where they face the problems of cultural conflict? Many of them have accumulated sufficient money to return to Punjab, where they can start afresh and live comfortably for the rest of their lives among their friends and relatives, but they continue to stay in England.

Rationale for staying

Almost all Punjabis in England aspire to eventually return home permanently, but they have been saying that since the day they arrived, in some cases for twenty years. Very few return to India, and a still smaller percentage stay there. In Jandiali, only four men have returned; three were old, and the fourth was from a wealthy family. Those in Gravesend who contemplate going back to settle in the village are afraid they will lose money on poor investments. Besides, they are not acclimatized to the unbearable heat. 'The beer is not as good', and 'I am not used to the primitive life any more' are common comments. When sixteen-year-old Karnail Singh returned to Punjab along with his parents and sister, they lived in a modern house in Model Town, Jullundur. However, Karnail was very unhappy. This was in sharp contrast to his sister, who was only a year his junior. Karnail was bored. He had a hard time at school in Jullundur because most of the classes were conducted in Gurmukhi. His Punjabi was not good. He did not make friends easily and was ignorant of peer habits. His failure to excel in *Kabaddi* compounded his problems. In England, it was easy for him to get a part-time job, but in Punjab caste restrictions prohibited employment at a clothing store or anywhere else for a Jat boy. Karnail's sister was content. In England, her life had been quite sheltered, and so she did not miss the freedom she had never experienced. She had worked with her mother, participated in women's functions, and associated with Punjabi girls, just as she was now doing in Punjab. Thus, Karnail wanted to return to England as soon as he came of age.

Young England-returnees find it especially hard to study in an institution where the medium of instruction is Punjabi. They are weary during vacation, because they are not allowed to get odd jobs to pass the time as they could in England. They have problems adjusting to their peers, who have not matured from an experience abroad; and they do not make friends readily. Girls, whose lives are basically centred around the home, have fewer adjustment problems. They are quite content to rejoin their old group of girl friends; only, those girls who have been to universities in England experience similar problems to those of Karnail Singh.

Often Gravesend–Jandiali migrants do not admit their will-
ingness to stay in England. Most rationalize staying on to save
face in spite of their being unhappy in Britain. Others claim
that it is too late to return to Punjab. However, there are a few
who admit to the charms of English life, chief among which are
the high and regular wages.

The welfare state also makes staying in England attractive.
Unemployment insurance, old-age pensions, and welfare benefits provide a security which is unheard of in India. A farmer
who has faced the threat of drought, famine, and bad prices
year after year appreciates not having the Sword of Damocles
hanging over his head. Although the installation of tube-wells,
irrigation, and tractors make Punjabi rural life more secure,
there is always the possibility of disaster. Parents returning with
teenage children do not usually go back to the village, but
settle in the urban areas of Jullundur and Hoshiarpur. Women
often discourage their husbands from returning to the joint-
family system. They do not want to be under the surveillance
of the whole village. There are other reasons also for desiring to
stay in England.

Village life is unbearable for the woman who has spent a few
years in England with modern conveniences in the kitchen and
bathroom. Cooking over an open fire, washing clothes on the
floor, cooking for the labourers, not having public transport or
a car, and defecating in fields rather than in toilets with a flush
system are all seemingly small factors, but when added up
they are important for an ex-émigré wife. It is almost impossible
for her to survive the hard life of a village girl after being used
to the gas and electrical appliances in Britain.

Binder Kaur was happy in England, and when her husband
talked about returning to Punjab, she quickly convinced him
to stay. Her persuasion did not have to be vehement, however,
for both Binder and her husband liked their privacy in England.
True, they were not strong without kinsmen, and it was lonely
sometimes. On the other hand, Binder did not have a mother-
in-law controlling her; she could run her house and raise her
children the way she pleased. They did not have the support of
the community in times of crisis, but they also did not have the
pressures of being accepted. She was not from the Doaba area,
so letters did not flood back to her home village as they did for

others. Binder and her family liked this new freedom to behave and spend their money as they desired, without the interference of parents, in-laws, or other family members.

Privacy has become a strong motivating factor to stay in England, again more for the women than the men. In the village, and in India generally, the concept of privacy as known in the west is virtually non-existent. Apart from the fact that it is customary for sons and their families to live with parents, which usually results in severe overcrowding, neighbours take great interest in one another's affairs and make it their business to know each others' wages, savings account, what a person does in his spare time, and where he or she goes. Nothing is private or too personal in the village. After the émigré has experienced privacy in England, he has no desire to relinquish it. And, if the mother-in-law follows the young couple to England, she is relegated to a secondary position because she is now in her daughter-in-law's house. Furthermore, each woman who holds a job acquires a more powerful position, undreamt of in the village. Both in Punjab and in England, the man who owns the house is the master and his wife the mistress, regardless of age.

The main disadvantage of this privacy and independence is the accompanying lack of security. If an immigrant is to have moral and financial support in times of need, he must keep strong village and blood ties. Some privacy must be sacrificed for survival. The Sikh must be part of his community, which exposes him and his household to the scrutiny and judgement of his peers. In England there appears to be a proportional relationship: the greater the number of kinsmen and friends, the better the sense of security. However, privacy and independence are curtailed. Conversely, fewer kinsmen means privacy and independence with diminished security.

Sikh Jats also like the nutritious food in England and boast of their improved health from the food, whiskey and beer. Thakur Singh was a sixty-year-old man who came to England to visit his only son and family. He was gray-haired, wrinkled, and weighed approximately 145 pounds, although he was a prosperous farmer, owning fifty acres of land in Punjab. Within two years, his physical appearance had changed so remarkably that when he went to the Indian High Commission in London to renew his passport, the passport officer did not believe that

9

the man in the old passport picture and the man in front of him were the same. Despite Thakur's honest demeanour, and against precedent, the official made the old Jat undress and show his birthmarks to prove he was the same man. The old Sikh in the picture had gained a good twenty-five pounds, dyed his hair and beard, and looked ten years younger. Jokingly, he told the passport officer (who he claims was a vegetarian Brahmin): 'My health has improved upon coming to England because my son feeds me chicken every week and I thrive on the excellent beer and Scotch!' The improved appearance of such returnees makes their contemporaries long to migrate to the land of milk and honey.

It is urban, professional Punjabis who are most disappointed upon arrival in England, especially lawyers[1] whose credentials are not recognized, and teachers who do not receive credit for past training and experience. Some admit that their expectations were too high and wish that they had never come, especially since they have neither family ties nor property in England.

Punjabis who attempt to return to India permanently do not fare well; many lose their wealth by making poor investments. Instead of staying in the village, they start a business in the city, where they are neither familiar with the local ways nor with the competition. Most of them return to England to recoup their losses. Balwant Singh is such a person. He came to England from a small village in Punjab. After three years in England, he returned with considerable savings. Being an England-returnee, Balwant felt superior and more knowledgeable than his village-mates, so he opened a store in the city of Jullundur. Since he knew nothing about retail buying and bargaining for proper prices, he quickly lost his savings. He returned to England to try again. Not having relied originally on village-mates whom he could trust, Balwant Singh had to accept the consequences and lose his earnings to people who had no concern for his welfare. Now in Gravesindia, Balwant Singh is planning to return to New Delhi and start a luggage shop in a year or so.[2]

Life in Punjab, although glorified in England, does not suit the migrant, who has become unaccustomed to the hot sun, spicy food, and poor sanitary conditions. Children born in England do not have the same kind of physical immunity as children born in the village. Hence, before long the English-returnee and his children become ill. Yet there is a real exhilaration in returning to Punjab and being respected by everyone. Being able to pay for other people, to buy lavish presents, and to be independent of the financial control of others, all give them a sense of elation as they walk down the streets of their community in India. And these few weeks of esteem are sometimes enough to justify slaving for several years in England.

The goals for many of the Gravesend–Jandiali migrants are beginning to shift in priority, which also makes returning unlikely. Wealth and an easy life are, for many, becoming ends in themselves. And the Gravesindians are prepared to make a great many sacrifices to gain more money.

To put it differently, once the hold of the village has been broken, wealth and privacy assume much higher value. Security within the kin group is not as essential as before, given the English system of national health and social services. However, a Punjabi does not completely fit into English society, so a compromise must be sought. But the Gravesindians feel they are trapped. As one Sikh said: 'We have chosen the frosting without the cake; and we cannot help ourselves.' In other words, some aspects of English life are enticing to the Punjabi, and he readily accepts them, but he feels he is forsaking the more important cultural traits for that which is easy and comfortable. Thus, very few Gravesindians readily admit that they will stay in England permanently.

Combating British influence

Though prepared to make a great many sacrifices and compromises in the search for wealth,[3] the Jats are at the same time searching for means to prevent their numbers from being absorbed into the host society. The English are perceived as a force destructive of Punjabi culture. Many of the norms used to maintain Sikh Jat beliefs have already been discussed; discipline from the village, influence of women, social control and hospitality according to the Punjabi concept of service, maintenance of family izzat, and abhorrence of certain British cultural traits. The Gravesindian community's prime concern is how to keep their children from adopting those traits of British culture that counter the teachings of the gurus and other Punjabi Sikh Jat cultural values and beliefs. The adults may compromise, but they want their children to be what they consider pure Sikhs.

According to them, problems with children in England are far greater than in Jandiali because of the direct influence of the English. Schools pose the main difficulty, because they teach children about western dating customs, love marriages, and also make them succumb to English peer-group pressure over unquestioned obedience to the parents.

The Jandiali–Gravesend migrants seek to minimize the influence of British culture by promoting Punjabi culture as a superior alternative. When their children do not respond to this approach, other means, including coercion, are used. The major tactics employed are: (1) minimizing contact with the English, (2) social control, (3) emotional blackmail, (4) defending Punjabi culture, and (5) discouraging emulation of British ways.

In the Gravesindians' search to minimize British influence on their children, segregation emerges as a possible solution. One proposal, mentioned earlier, was to start a Khalsa school, a project which has not materialized. Children spend most of their waking hours with British teachers, who, according to the Gravesindians, actually demean Punjabi ways. Since the school problem is faced by all Sikh Jats in England and because of the large amount of capital needed, a nationwide Punjabi effort would be required to start a Sikh school; for Gravesend alone could not support such a venture.

The only way to remove their children from the influence of the English school teacher is to send them back to Punjab for education. Some have gone to boarding schools in the hill stations, others to stay with relatives in cities. This is indeed an expensive venture, both monetarily and emotionally. Extensive contact with Punjab and India are considered by some Gravesindians as the only means to combat British cultural influences.

The other alternative for the Gravesindians who cannot afford to, or prefer not to, send children to India is close chaperoning. Although restricting freedom is more vital for girls than for boys, it is practised extensively in both cases. Girls and boys are encouraged to walk to school in groups of their own sex; sisters are encouraged to be close friends and to support one another. Many parents watch from a discreet distance, without the child's knowledge, and only if the child deviates does the parent take appropriate action.

When it is time for graduation to secondary school, capable Sikh Jat girls are withdrawn from school with the excuse that they are needed at home, in the family business, or as additional wage-earners. Whether they like it or not, these girls obey dutifully. Only two Gravesindian girls went to college via the grammar school; the rest were not allowed to enter secondary school for fear they would desire a higher education and taste independence.

Older boys out of school are also encouraged to go in groups, and the Indian Youth Federation was formed to keep young boys together and out of trouble. Community elders encouraged this organization as a source of friends for their boys and as a purposeful channel for youthful energy. The gurdwara also sponsors the Gurdwara Sports Federation, which caters to youth, encouraging Punjabi boys to compete throughout England in *Kabaddi* matches and other sporting events. The sports programme is a major item in the gurdwara budget.

The young are the concern of everyone, and the Sikhs feel parents should certainly be informed if their child behaves improperly. For example, a Punjabi girl on her way home from town once spoke to one of the boys she had grown up with. Upon reaching home, she was confronted by her parents, who had received a telephone call about her behaviour, and was told in no uncertain terms that she should never speak to boys. Communal gossip and criticism can be vicious among the Gravesindians, and since news travels fast to the home village and back again, everyone knows the others' business. Even if not felt inwardly, an outward appearance of obedience to cultural dictates must be kept.

When Dalip Kaur's son married an English girl, she cried and wailed among her Punjabi friends, outwardly manifesting great sorrow, but privately, and to her English neighbours, she admitted her approval. When questioned by a close friend about her double standards, Dalip Kaur replied: 'My son is promoting good race relations and we are happy, but if I show my joy, I will be ostracized and criticized by my community and friends, and we cannot afford this, being so far away from home.'

Dalip Kaur, her husband, and their two-month-old son, Jatinder, came to Gravesend before there were many Punjabis there. Jati was raised like the other English boys; he topped the list for the eleven plus exams and went from grammar school to university. Both Dalip Kaur and her husband were extremely proud of him. They did not deny their son anything. The boy had only been in India once and was more a part of English culture than Punjabi. Dalip Kaur admits that they tried to be strict with Jati after other Jats started coming to Gravesend, but the boy was already deeply committed to English ways. Being a boy was to his advantage and he was able to get away with much more than had he been a girl. Neither Dalip Kaur nor her husband want to lose their son. Not only is he their security for later years, but they love him and are willing to welcome his English wife into the family.

A Kenyan Asian had another experience which reflects the feelings of Gravesindian parents in raising their daughters. Biro Kaur worked at a zipper factory and, because of her hard work, the manager decided to hire other Punjabi girls to work there. One day on the way home on the bus, the young Punjabi girls (fresh out of school) were sitting together; they were jabbering in Punjabi, giggling loudly, thus bothering the English ladies who were tired from a hard day's work. Consequently, Biro told the girls that instead of sitting in groups, they should separate and sit beside the English ladies to improve their English and learn British ways. Coming from Kenya, her thinking was different from those from India, and she did not weigh the ramifications of such a suggestion. Apparently, one of the young girls went home and told her mother what Biro had said. Half a dozen mothers were at her doorstep that weekend and told her not to spoil their daughters by encouraging them to adopt English ways and become like herself. If they heard more of her western ideas from their daughters, they would take action against her.

In Gravesindia, behaviour is a mutual responsibility. If a wayward child's parents cannot control him, they seek the advice and help of other members of the community, usually a village-mate or a kinsman. When Darshan Singh's son started stealing and issuing false bank cheques, he went to his good friend, Kuldip Singh, for advice. Kuldip and his father, along with another village-mate, Fakir Singh, carefully deliberated the problem, talked to the lad, and tried to find a way to straighten him out before he affected his father's reputation any further.

Gravesindians want their children to have a strong desire to uphold parental values. This desire results from the concept of a child's obligation to his parents or believing the Sikh Jat way to be the best. Parents frequently endeavour to make a child feel obliged by playing on his guilt and using emotional black-mail.[4] A mother may say to her son, 'If you marry a white girl, our family izzat will be harmed so drastically that I will be forced to commit suicide.' Most commonly, however, a mother pleads 'poor health' or claims 'to be dying' because of the deviant behaviour of a son or daughter. The responsibility for deviancy lies heavily on both sexes. A younger sister's marriage arrangements may be hindered if the older sister behaves im-properly; even cousins are affected socially by a relative's improper behaviour. The child learns early about these re-percussions. To harm those who have loved and nurtured one is unworthy, and the guilt for the death of a parent or grand-parent is too high a price to pay.

Another tactic is for parents to grant every wish of their son in the hope that, when the father is unable to earn good wages, the grateful boy will uphold his family responsibility and care for his elders. Unlike young people in western society, who, because of the early thrust toward independence and marriage must strive hard to get a start in life, the newly married Pun-jabi couples are adequately provided for by their parents. The young couple have time to know and adjust to one another and they can start their family free of financial worries. A son, grateful to his parents for their generosity, respects them and their wishes in old age.

In an effort to keep their children close, Gravesindians glorify Sikh Jat culture, especially during gurdwara services, when the martyrdom and sacrifices of early Sikhs and their gurus are constantly praised. The point is continually made that the Sikhs in England should also be willing to sacrifice for Sikhism, keep their unshaven hair, and live up to the dictates of their faith. Some families tell their children tales of glory of famous Sikhs from history and legend. This is to make the child proud of his symbols and willing to wear them honourably, with his head held high.

In defending the practice of arranged marriages, one well-educated Punjabi offered a persuasive argument.

My son has nothing to worry about except his studies, to which he can devote his full attention. When he comes of age and is ready, we will find him a suitable girl who will make him very happy. All these English boys think about is sex and girls, and due to family pressures, rush into marriage. Boys and girls in English society marry at a very early age without the boy having sufficient resources and a good education, so he ends up as a common labourer. According to our Punjabi way, our boys can concentrate on making a success out of their life because they have no worries or pressures. When a young man picks out his own wife at an early age, he is thinking only of sex. When my wife and I select a girl for our son, we look at the overall picture—the family, psychological compatibility, and maturity of the girl. And, we consider all these aspects objectively. Our children are free, as they do not have to suffer from the emotional trauma of being responsible for finding their future spouse. They know their parents will do the best possible job.

Most girls trust their parents fully to find the best possible match. Young men generally know that the parents want them to have good wives, and entrust their parents with the responsibility. Although there were exceptions elsewhere in England, in Gravesindia young boys and girls generally continue to rely on their parents to arrange their marriages.

In an effort to discourage their children from emulating the British, some parents instil fear by referring to the Englishman as the 'bogey man'. When a child misbehaves, he is commonly threatened with being given to the *gora*. Other children are taught contempt. A white man and his family accepted an invitation to a Punjabi neighbour's home. When they entered the house, the little four-year-old daughter screamed in terror and ran from the room, huddling in a corner of the kitchen near a stove. Repeated coaxing and pleading would not encourage her to act properly. It was learned that her parents had told her that if she was bad the *gora* would take her away, and she thought her end had come. Even though the little Punjabi girl went to school and played with the English neighbour's daughter, she would not go to their house because she was afraid of her friend's father.

In another situation, my wife attended an *akhand path* with some of her Punjabi friends. Since she had lived in the United States for ten years, she was often thought to be European rather than a Punjabi. Upon entering the hostess's home, the eleven-year-old daughter using a contemptuous tone asked her mother in Punjabi, 'What is that *gori* doing here?' To her, this was a Sikh ceremony and the whites were not welcome.

So strongly are such values imprinted on the minds of the young that they find it extremely difficult, often impossible, to be free of them, even when they are intellectually convinced of their irrelevance. As one Punjabi college student confessed:

I have been taught in college that sexual freedom is acceptable, that living with a girl without being married to her is permissible, and intellectually I cannot refute their arguments, but inside me I know that they are wrong. Therefore, I prefer a village girl who is a virgin and will obey me, love me, and look after me rather than an English girl who may flirt with other boys and may even divorce me at the slightest argument.

EPILOGUE
(1972-1978)

The Gravesindians have been a community in England for almost thirty years. Over forty-five per cent of their numbers were born in England and are technically British citizens. However, it is not clear in the minds of either the Sikhs or the host society as to whether the new generation are English, Punjabis, or immigrants. They are labelled 'immigrants' by the host community, when by birth they are subjects of the Queen of England. Although they will probably never return to their home land, they claim to be 'Indian' or 'Punjabi'. Neither the host community nor the Punjabis themselves refer to the community as being 'English'. In spite of the ambivalent position, the Gravesindians have continued to maintain their identity and culture. They have successfully been able to instil both in their children.

Even though these villagers are severely criticized by both the English and the urban Indians for not mixing with the host community, their situation is such that they really cannot. However, maintaining ethnic separation has certain advantages for the Gravesindians. By remaining apart from their hosts, they are able to keep their pride and identity. They are still Sikh Jat landowners, and not unskilled labourers in the lower stratum of English society. Having this sense of pride and worth certainly gives Gravesindians confidence in themselves. The immigrant works hard, determines communal and individual life-goals, and retains a self-respect which is essential to the well-being of any person. Because of this separateness, the Sikh Jats feel no inhibitions about keeping their businesses open longer hours, or working on weekends to make better money. They have also cast aside certain strictures of Punjabi culture and have accepted jobs as janitors and airport terminal cleaners, jobs they would never do in Punjab.

The problems of these Punjabis have also undergone change. Their initial concerns had focused on finding housing and jobs

but now they concentrate on their children. Many of t[...]
regarding their girls and boys discussed during the [...]
debate' have become a reality, and they are anxious about
losing the Punjabi Sikh culture. They worry about girls leaving
the family and shaming the kin group. There is a deep feeling
of vulnerability and, as one Indian stated, 'insecurity breeds
aggression'.

There are other circumstances that add to their unsureness,
like the Asian expulsion from Uganda, Margaret Thatcher's
call for a clear end to immigration, and the subsequent rise of
the National Front. The latter, a Nazi-type party openly
promoting anti-immigrant sentiments, has grown in prominence and proposes to participate strongly in coming elections.
Ironically, Mr Lane, a conservative who the Asians claim has
made several anti-immigrant statements, was appointed as head
of the Commission for Racial Equality, formerly called the
Community Relations Commission, a government concern with
a goal for promoting racial harmony in Britain. Interestingly,
however, the Commission has only won 8 of 50 cases investigated under the 1976 Race Relations Act. This poor score
augments the lack of faith the Jats may have had in the Commission, and they perceive themselves in an assailable situation,
thus making it more difficult to decide on how to deal with
their future.

If one were to greatly simplify the situation in describing
Gravesindia, 'tension' would be an appropriate adjective. The
psychological stress is manifest in the approximately 40 per
cent increase in heart problems and about a 50 per cent increase
in the use of tranquillizer-type drugs among the community.
Social strains are first discovered in the private discussions and
debates within the community. These anxieties are largely
caused by the change in the composition of the Sikh community; by Ugandan and Kenyan refugees, more spouses after
the new legislation permitting both boys and girls to be sponsored for marriages, and second generation children coming
into prominence. As the following example will show, Kenyan
and Ugandan Asians have socially less conservative ideas than
the Jat Gravesindians. At the conclusion of a meeting in 1977
of the local Community Relations Council, the last item on the
agenda was 'any other business'. Balvinder Singh, a Kenyan

Asian, was recognized and introduced an emotional issue. 'We need a place where Indian boys and girls can meet. We need a place where our girls can get together and be free of the unfair restrictions of their parents.' Tempers flared, and the debate was on. One village segment advocated *purdah*-like restrictions so that their daughters would remain pure and upright. A westernized and Kenyan group argued that modern ideas must be considered and that girls had a right to equality and freedom like the males. There was also an element who advocated a position between the two extremes.

The issue of girls continues to be a concern in Gravesend. Some promote freedom, while others are afraid that the liberal behaviour of their daughters will harm family izzat. But, in this debate, a fresh aspect was introduced. The East African Asians, of whom Balvinder Singh is a member, are often more lenient. They allow their girls to wear western dress (some bare their legs) and are not intimidated by the dictates of Jat villagers. The East African Asians, who are generally professionally oriented, tend to move into and fit into British neighbourhoods, whereas the village migrants prefer their own localities and maintain social barriers between themselves and the host community. The Ugandan Asians have undergone one forced evacuation and do not want to go through another, which makes them more irascible to unfair treatment in Britain. The village Jats disapprove of East African Asian liberalism and disagree about the actions to be followed by the community.

Parents are finding that bringing spouses from the village to marry a child who has resided in England leads to adjustment problems. If a boy comes from the village, he expects his wife to cook at any time convenient to him, which may mean that a girl who is working full time might have to wake up in the middle of the night and serve her husband who has just returned from the pub. He expects her to walk behind him, keep her head covered and behave modestly, just like a village wife. Dimpal Kaur was recently married to a village boy. Dimpal, however, had been in England for the past ten years. One night when her husband's friend came to the door, she yelled, 'Gurbachan, your friend is here'. That night she was severely chastised; village wives never refer to their husbands by their first names, and Dimpal must not do so either, especially in public. The Gravesindian girl who has been raised in England is unfamiliar with these practices. Besides, she has learned that females should have certain rights, especially if they are bringing in a pay cheque. This creates a clash in expected behaviour, both for Punjabi boys and girls exposed to the western lifestyle.

Bhola Singh lived in England for about ten years, and then married a girl from the village. Having been raised in England and been acquainted with the western concept of love and compatibility, he desired the same type of relationship with his wife, but whenever Bhola Singh tried to be romantic or affectionate with his wife, she became flustered and did not understand what was happening. To her, sex was necessary only for procreation. Whenever Bhola tried to share his inner feelings with her, or discuss philosophy and social goals, she had no comprehension of what he was trying to say, but dutifully listened without disagreeing or interacting. Bhola soon began to see that the relationship he had hoped for was impossible.

The role definitions and expectations of marriage partners greatly differ between the village and Gravesindia. In village Punjab, a couple may be compatible, but the sharing of the inner self is not with one's spouse but with members of one's own sex. Western romantic notions are unheard of and not generally part of the Indian's scope of marriage. Thus, a boy or girl from a rural area has no idea about what the Punjabi raised in England is trying to accomplish in a marriage relationship. The couple cannot communicate anything deeper than the shallow meaning of verbal exchange. If one party raised in England tries to be demonstrative in their affections, the person from the village becomes nervous, irritable, and unresponsive. They do not understand the partner's behaviour and interpret it as exploitation, leading to frustration and sadness for both. Divorce is seldom resorted to—they just go through life mutually tolerant of one another.

The tensions created by bringing spouses from a village are due to more than just role expectation. As Ajay Singh discovered, the power balance in the kin group becomes one-sided. Ajay Singh was brought from Banga to wed Preminder Kaur, a Jat girl raised in England. Her family paid for his ticket, but gave no other dowry. They lived in joint residence with her family, but the criticism of him by her parents was so great that they moved to a house down the street. Preminder's relatives visited daily and said 'Ajay is lazy; look how slow he is in fixing up the house' or 'Ajay is a sloppy worker. See, the wallpaper is not matched neatly'. Preminder had conflicting loyalties between her husband and her parents. She felt that her future resided in him. But her parents and brothers felt that if Ajay did not behave properly they would send him back to India and marry Preminder to another boy, for girls with British passports bring handsome matches even from wealthy doctors in Jullundur and other areas of Punjab.

In Punjab, a boy who stays in his wife's home is derogatorily termed a *ghar-javai* or a house son-in-law. It is implied that he cannot support himself or does not come from a good home where he can take his wife. There is disrespect for such a person in Punjabi culture. Therefore, a boy sponsored from the village to England is in an assailable position. He has no family to help him and is at the mercy of his in-laws. Besides, the opportunity to come to England forces him to live up to the expectations of his family—that is, make money and send some home, and sponsor relatives.

The girl raised in England is torn between loyalty to her family and her husband. The two loyalties are next to impossible—she eventually must choose or end up living a life pleasing neither. The bride brought from the village is also a sad case. In Punjab, if she is treated improperly, she has her brothers or father to help her. Or, if she is married with a good dowry, she is in a position of respect. In England, she has no one and again is completely at the mercy of her in-laws—a sad situation, for often the tactic is to be hyper-critical of the new bride to keep her humble. The new bride lacks self-confidence and is unsure of herself. Being from the village, her parents may not have been able to give a sufficient dowry to gain the regard of Punjabis in England. She comes into her new family from a position of weakness unless an immigrant uncle or aunt has given her a 'posh' marriage.

Sikh parents in Britain generally want to have their children married at an early age. They know that once the child has tasted independence, he is less likely to remain under their control and probably will not consent to a 'good marriage' because he will not accept their choice. Girls, especially, are married fairly young and discouraged from going to a university. It is not so simple to marry off the boy soon so that he will remain dependent. However, most immigrant parents choose to wait until the son's professional training is complete and he is established before the union is arranged.

There is further conflict as to whom the marriage should be to. As one lady stated, 'We could have married our daughter to a doctor, but we had to fulfil my husband's family obligations and marry her to an ignorant villager.' Gravesindians had often made commitments in their home region for marriages. Or, they had been giving their daughters or receiving girls from certain families for a long period and had to honour those commitments. British passport holders can name their marriage price and choose from among professionals in India.

The generation division takes other forms. For instance, when the National Front was campaigning in Gravesend to promote their cause, the different generations were divided as to how to cope with the situation. Some elders felt that conciliation and negotiation were the answer. The youth felt the threat and reacted in kind—organizing themselves to 'meet force with force'. Their argument was, 'We are not going to let them molest our women.' Generally, the elders took the conciliatory line, while the youngsters, led by the Indian Youth Federation, were the militants.

Stories of Asian girls running away from home to escape an arranged marriage or to wed a boy not liked by the family periodically headline the British press. An article in 1977 described a father murdering his daughter because she wanted to marry a West Indian boy. Such a union was not approved of by either family or community. Social workers and Community Relations Officers often have horror stories of Punjabi girls suffering under the oppression of their families. These are not limited to marriage, but include girls who may want to further their education but are forbidden to proceed because they are of marriageable age.

Social workers in Britain uphold the value of individualism and fail to understand or condone the Punjabi concept of subordinating individual will for family honour. In some places social workers have set up homes for runaway Asian girls. Such a venture has been considered in Gravesend, but is vigorously opposed by the Punjabis. They do not feel that British social workers should assume or undermine parental authority. There is tension as to how the British social services should deal with such situations and to what degree cultural relativism should be condoned in England.

For the girl, even marriage does not allow her to escape from parental pressure. Kanwal Kaur was married when she was being trained as a nurse. However, her husband agreed to let her continue her training and take birth control pills. After several months, her mother wondered why Kanwal was not pregnant. Searching through her daughter's room, she discovered the pills and flushed them down the toilet. One month later, Kanwal was pregnant and much to her chagrin had to drop out of the training programme.

When a girl does not become pregnant soon after marriage, people wonder about the success and consummation of the marriage. Kanwal's mother was worried, and to prove to the community that her daughter had a perfect marriage, she acted in the manner she thought correct. Kanwal's intentions had to be subordinated for the benefit of the family.

Boys also have problems, and as one lad stated:

I love art and want to study it more, but father wants me to learn physics and chemistry, for those professions lead one to better paying jobs. In the end, I know that his desires will dominate.

Gravesindians, like most South Asians, view an education to be worthless unless it can be used to make a good living. Accounting is a popular field for many Asian youths in England because not only does it bring in a good wage, but has potential both in England and India. Besides, it is a field for making one independent (by starting one's own firm), and is culturally prestigious. Sciences, engineering, and medicine are also highly approved of. Unfortunately for the non-scientific minds, Gravesindian elders consider the social sciences or philosophy a useless education. Thus, when a Gravesindian youth decides to study something other than a money-making profession, the parents disapprove, resulting in a clash of goals with the youth ultimately conforming to parental wishes.

The elders have their tactics to bring about compliance. A

father continually reminds his son that if he does not study, he will have to do shift work all his life. Every young man is aware that education is the one means of breaking out of his low class situation in British society. When persuasion fails, parents resort to the effectiveness of emotional blackmail. As mentioned in earlier chapters, no son wants to cause pain to his mother.

Gravesindians are realizing, however, that sending children to India for schooling is not a viable alternative. The youth suffer from poor health due to the difference in diet, they miss the amenities of English life, and are ill adjusted to the strictures of village grandparents and Indian boarding schools. The sports activities, medium of instruction, and behavioural norms of India become more and more alien to the child raised in England. There is also the emotional and physical trauma of sending a child to India, and the practice, though still resorted to, is becoming infrequent.

Whether or not a child shares parental values, there is a general obedience to their authority in regulating behaviour. This does not imply that there is no questioning or disagreement with the elders, but rebellion and disobedience are less common than among their western counterparts. Because of parental control, these second generation Jats in England do not pose a problem for the social services. Delinquency and crime among the Asian youth in Gravesend is minimal—only two or three cases have been reported of petty shop-lifting involving Punjabis. Asian youth have an excellent reputation for performing well in school. The parents may be uneducated, but they ensure that their children do their school work and closely supervise the offspring's time and life so that studies are given top priority.

Punjabi elders are always aware of communal opinion and are concerned about bad conduct. A phone call from a disapproving member of the community is given credence, and the culprit child is restricted and chastised. Gravesindians control each other by gossip. Obedience to peer evaluation is so internalized that it is blindly adhered to. This stems from a concern for arranging proper marriages and maintaining a high family izzat.

The child who deviates suffers the most. Daulat Singh is a young boy in college who feels out of place because of his long hair. His parents have instilled in him that Sikhs should not

10

trim the beard. Although it is not noticeable to an Englishman, members of the Punjabi community have said to his father, 'I notice Daulat is shaving'. Daulat's father is heart-broken. He came to England and sacrificed many good jobs because he believed that a Sikh should keep his turban. Daulat's behaviour has destroyed all that the family has stood for, and the elder's health is deteriorating. The father feels ashamed when he looks at other members in the community, for all that he has dedicated his life to is lost by his son's action.

The father did not object to his son's behaviour until it was mentioned among other Gravesindians. The key factor is not the behaviour, but how the behaviour is perceived and evaluated by the group. Many Gravesindian parents know that their children deviate, but only become really concerned when they think that other Punjabis will learn of the misconduct—which is most of the time. Deviancy is almost always discovered. A child who does not uphold parental values brings sadness. The deterioration of health in a parent is sometimes more than just play-acting to instil guilt; it actually does happen.

There is, however, the reverse kind of situation, as in Arjun Singh's case—a teenager whose father had shaved and concentrated on working hard to make money. While visiting Punjab, Arjun came under the influence of his orthodox uncle, who persuaded the boy to wear a turban, regrow his hair, and become a good Sikh. Upon returning to England, Arjun convinced his father to grow his hair. Now the elder claims that 'when I was shaven I was weak and sickly. Now, I have good health and am strong, due to my long hair.' Arjun is proud of his symbols and claims that 'if the *goras* ridicule me, I will show them who is strong'.

Arjun achieved a meaning and purpose in life through the influence of his uncle, and is also a top student in his class. He strives to prove to others the superiority of the real Sikhs. His 'conversion' has also influenced his father, who has become a *pukka* or 'true' Sikh again. For the second generation, once a set of values become internalized, they are very strong in maintaining them and living up to their cultural heritage. Arjun's situation seems to be gaining popularity in the community. More men are growing their beards than before, and to be a Sikh is taking on greater pride. As people grow older and the

community progresses through time, there is a resurgence of
ethnic pride, and being a Punjabi Sikh Jat is taking on a higher
meaning and greater significance for individuals and the society
as a whole. For a period in their lives, some young Punjabi
immigrants pass off as Spanish and Italian, hiding their identity
and anglicizing their names. But, in adulthood, names become
Indianized again, and the memories of youth are more appealing. This is typified in the following comments of one Punjabi
who grew up in Britain.

Life in my youth was crowded, as we lived jointly in our house. There
were many people around, meals were served at odd hours, and
company was always popping in and disrupting plans. But that kind
of life was very enjoyable. Now I lead an orderly life, have privacy,
and guard these things. But I do not like what is happening to me.
There was something pleasant about the crowded days of my youth
where pandemonium was the norm.

Some of the tensions of second generation Gravesindians are
difficult to fully understand. There are many variables; type of
upbringing, and reaction to return visits to India are but two of
them. Generally, Sikh youth adopts a behavioural pattern that
lies somewhere between complete rejection or complete acceptance of village norms and goals. There are some who are
aware of a cultural vacuum. This is best explained in an analogy
by a young girl who pointed to a new, but vacant, house and
said,

See that new house? It is beautiful on the outside, but there is nothing
inside. That is the way it is with us westernized Indians. We wear
Indian clothes, but there is nothing inside. We feel an emptiness that
is only relieved by being active.

A few second generation Punjabis (usually of urban origin or
with a westernized education) have 'nothing inside'. That is,
their parents have been so busy working that the children have
neither learned Gurmukhi nor absorbed Punjabi goals, values,
and means. Such an emptiness often leads to certain behavioural consequences whereby an individual works hard and
becomes overly active—anything to occupy himself so that he
does not face the emptiness within. As one young man, who
had committed himself to Indian norms, said:

Look at Raj; he continually goes to parties and the pub. This is a way

in which he escapes from the inner emptiness he feels when he is alone.
I feel sorry for him.

Others suffer from a feeling of deep insecurity which is manifested in aggressiveness toward the host society. Whether justi-
fied or not, the British are perceived as aliens to be fought
against, thus lending purpose or fulfilment to an otherwise
empty life.

Most Punjabi youngsters, however, have been exposed to
Punjabi culture to such an extent that they are not 'empty
inside'. The authoritarian family structure has been maintained; these young Gravesindians have a goal to work for,
even if it is dictated by their elders. But for them, there is a
source of confusion, for in school they are taught Christian and
western norms, which often contradict Sikh Jat teachings, thus
leading to indecision as to which system to adhere.

The following testimony of a young girl illustrates the results
of different child-rearing practices.

Why should I go to the gurdwara? I cannot understand it when they
read out of the Holy Book; and, even if I could, the women are so
busy gossiping that I can't hear anything. It is different for Jagira;
her parents raised her in a strict manner. She learned to read the
Granth Sahib; it means something to her.

Jagira is one of those who has been taught their religion and
culture and accepts it (accepting the teachings is crucial).
Therefore, the emptiness is not as pronounced as it might have
been had she lost her Sikhism. The keen sense of being a misfit
in British society continually generates a psychological conflict.
Those who have not internalized an ideological system are
blown to and fro by the wind; they emulate one set of behaviour
without fully understanding the deep significance of their actions. They aimlessly copy others belonging to their environment without a full commitment to any ideological position.

The second generation Gravesindians talk about returning
to India. They have been taught a glorified version of village
life, and when they do return to their home village, they realize
they cannot settle in India; a fact they only admit privately or
reveal in remarks like, 'There is no flush system in the village'
or 'I can't stand seeing beggars' and 'There is no privacy'. Like
their elders, these youngsters are ignorant of India's urban

opportunities and view South Asia in terms of their village. Few Punjabi immigrants, if any, decide to return to India on a permanent basis.

A lack of belonging has to be faced by second generation Gravesindians. It is more than just being different and considered strange by the host community, or being discriminated against and ridiculed. Their behaviour differs according to cultural norms. This is best illustrated in a conversation one evening when an Indian migrant began talking about his return to Punjab:

It felt so good to be home in Punjab. That is where I belong. One day, while waiting in line to buy a bus ticket, a fellow got in front of me. I shoved him out of line and told him off. In England, I would never do such a thing to a white person, but would have passively accepted the situation.

Sheila, a young girl of mixed parentage, broke into the discourse and asked: 'But, what do you do when you do not have a home?' Sheila voiced the dilemma of second generation Asians, who do not have a country—a place where they can belong and feel confident of themselves so that they can behave in adversity without being overly aggressive or meek. One return trip to rural Punjab vividly communicates to them that they no longer belong in India.

Therefore, whether they like it or not, the second generation Gravesindians have no choice—they must survive in England. They have to determine the method and goals for this survival. Unfortunately, they perceive that survival of the fittest is the only way, and aggression seems to be the most likely solution to be considered among the youth.

The elders return to the village periodically for a holiday and rejuvenation. Life in England is becoming tense and trying. And, although they will probably never return to Jandiali permanently, the village continues to be a place of fond memories. This is because they do not have to earn their livelihood in Punjab, and since they come home with pounds, which have a higher buying power in Punjab than in England, they can relax. In Jandiali, they have a sense of belonging and are held in high esteem; at least that is how they perceive themselves. Also, when they return to Gravesend, they tend to forget the unpleasant aspects and inconveniences of village life which the younger generation vividly remembers, especially since their own ties with the village are not strong.

The social barrier between the English and Punjabis in Gravesend was maintained until the time this study was completed. However, there are a few bicultural Indians who try and bridge the gap between the two communities by actively participating in Community Relations Councils and representing the whole immigrant group. The host group look toward these bicultural immigrants and are strongly influenced by their so-called representative opinions. These opinions do not necessarily or always coincide with those of the immigrant group at large. The remark of the government official that 'All one has to do is go to Thandi's Pub [owned by an Indian] and you will really learn about the Punjabi community' was an erroneous one. This informant did not realize that the Punjabis who haunt Thandi's Pub are not the leaders of the community nor true representatives. They are often held in disrepute by most Gravesindians. Brokers tell the hosts only what they feel the English like to hear, or since some of these Punjabis have political ambitions of their own, they use this pub to gain support from white leaders. The local CRC claims a 35 per cent emigrant membership, disregarding the fact that many of their Indian members and organizations have been inactive for over ten years. The leading Indian participants are primarily of urban orientation and do not reflect the needs and goals of their village counterparts. Local community relations organizations have reports and committee formations to testify to their accomplishments. Although papers do not always bring about intra-ethnic understanding, they are the major tactic used to gain legitimacy in the eyes of those who provide funds. The Community Relations Council of Gravesend is diligently trying to promote an understanding between the Asian and English communities and have an impressive record of accomplishments. However, they communicate mainly with the educated Gravesindians, thus failing to establish rapport between the common people of both cultures.

Some Gravesindian elders respect Britain and the integrity and honesty they think the country stands for; there are others who are not so sure. The dramatic rise of the National Front, with its emphasis on promoting anti-immigrant feelings and policies, has given many second thoughts. This was vividly brought home to them in 1976 when the National Front marched down the main street of Gravesend, defamed the walls of the gurdwara, and pushed the President of the Gurdwara Committee through a shop window. Jat women walking in town had their earrings pulled off and were abused. Indians and English in Gravesend all agree that this trouble was caused by outsiders,[1] but the effects of the demonstration linger on. One lady expressed this when she said, 'I must always take an early train home, for the National Front thugs hang out near the railway station.' The area of greatest conflict seems to be East London, which has always been a tension spot for new arrivals, and the events in this area are reported in the national press, affecting the feelings of Asians and English alike throughout the country.

The Gravesindian youngsters have a difficult time reconciling themselves to the animosity created by the host society. They have learned in school about high standards of morality and fair play in British culture, and are disappointed and hostile when they are not accorded these same rights. Thus, they sometimes look to organizations with Marxist-type revolutionary ideologies. It was during the National Front invasion in Gravesend that the youth, under the leadership of the Indian Youth Federation, were prepared to meet force with force. Their rallying slogan was 'We are not going to allow the Nazis to humiliate our women'. However, many people in Gravesend, English and Indian alike, worked hard and calmly to maintain peace in the city—which they accomplished remarkably well.

Even the elders are becoming belligerent. This was illustrated in Gravesend when a liaison officer was hired by the Gravesend school authorities. A study of the Gravesend school showed that Punjabi parents should be encouraged to be more familiar and interested in the schools. Gravesindians supervise their children's studies, but they seldom participate in school activities. It was decided that a liaison officer should be employed to visit Indian households and try to get them more involved in the Gravesend school programmes. Gravesindians were irate when they learned that the person chosen was a female Parsee who smoked, wore dresses, and spoke no Punjabi and little Hindi.

She exhibited behaviour that is inappropriate to Jat cultural norms. Thus, all the Indian organizations jointly petitioned against hiring her. At the time of writing, the wishes of the Punjabi community were being ignored by the authorities. But, what is significant is that Gravesindians united solidly on an issue that affected them.

The future of Gravesindians remains to be seen. It is safe to say that separateness will continue as a behavioural trait, encouraged by both the Punjabis and the British. How the Sikh Jat community will function internally can be gauged from the 'school debate'. Although the unified community will continue to oppose the British, further dissension will develop between the shaven, liberal Sikhs and their unshaven conservative counterparts. The latter are likely to fight more vehemently for maintaining Sikh symbols, separateness, and the Sikh faith. They will try to implement restrictions within the gurdwara (for example, only unshaven Sikhs may hold office) which will affect and influence the wider Gravesindian community. However, shaven Sikhs will attend and fully participate in Punjabi functions, and many may try to make their children more conservative or more Punjabi than they are. Other shaven Sikhs will not be so strict; they may allow their boys to date white girls, but control of the Punjabi females will always have high priority among these transplanted villagers.

Punjab will continue to be home for the next few generations, and glorification of the homeland will be strong, especially among those who have not returned to visit that area. Everyone will pay lip service to the plan to return, but will remain in Britain, since returning is not realistic.

One factor must be kept in mind—the militaristic tradition of the Sikh Jats. Although these people can be channelled toward constructive ends, the partition of India and the Punjabi Subha Movement indicate how this unified soldier-saint brotherhood can turn from a peaceful community to a volatile force. Heavy discrimination by the British host community can have disastrous results. Such violence is imminent in the future if the racial situation in Britain continues on its present course.

Primary immigration from Punjab to England has stopped, but the English of Gravesend and elsewhere have an underlying fear that the immigrants, especially those from India, are taking over their country. Spouses are still brought from India to marry Sikh Jats in England, and the youngster with a British passport commands an extremely high dowry or access to a family with considerable wealth and prestige in India. And it seems that for every spouse brought from India, thirty more relatives are apt to follow, since a person can sponsor parents, siblings, and their spouses, who can further invite siblings, and so the chain goes on. The arrival of the Ugandan Asians in 1972 instilled fear into the British public, for they now wonder if they are responsible for all non-white British passport holders throughout the Commonwealth. In other words, the host community wants to know if and when immigration to their country will stop. This view is held by many of the immigrants as well; except that they want their relatives exempted from the restrictions.

In Gravesend, Englishmen also feel that the Gravesindians are taking over. The Punjabi community has now grown to over 7,000 Asians.[2] They are also visible in the commercial activities of the community, a boom that began around 1974. Six of sixteen chemist shops are Indian-owned; four pubs, one automobile repair garage, a number of green grocers, two laundromats, one bicycle shop, one electric shop, five grocery stores, five driving schools, three market stalls, one children's boutique, one clothing factory, two construction companies, and one sweet shop comprised the Gravesindian business community in 1978.

Besides the eleven Asian doctors and one-third of the hospital staff being Indian, there are two accountants (and numerous trainees), twelve engineers (more than one working at the Ford Motor Company), two bank clerks, seven school teachers, two clerks at the Bureau Council, several clerks in the Post Office, one Indian social worker, and one occupational therapist. Compared with the situation in 1971, one can understand the feeling that the British have of the Indians taking over, especially since their distinctive dress and colour make the Asians appear more numerous than they actually are. And, because the Indian businessman is willing to stay open longer hours and live more frugally than his British competitors, he can often make a business that once was considered a failure, a success. However, the vast majority of Gravesindians still occupy unskilled jobs at the Ford Motor Company, Imperial Paper Company, and the Bowater-Scott Paper Company. The cement factory in neighbouring Northfleet and a nearby upholstery factory employ those who are willing to accept demanding jobs with odd hours. These positions are not as apparent as the business, medical, and professional workers, but they have their effect on the English.

There are also many things about Gravesindian behaviour that the host community does not understand. For example, one company had complaints of Asian workers relieving themselves on the toilet floor rather than using the sitter commode. Officials of the company, trying to be accommodating, installed a squatter toilet, for they had learned of the cultural aversion Indians have of using a sitter. The Punjabi employees, interpreting the installation of the squatter as being inferior to the English, smashed the squatter commode. The English managers were offended and bitter at this kind of response when they were trying to be accommodating. An occasional Indian workman will take advantage of the ignorance of a British foreman not to do his full share of work. For example, he will claim that sweeping is against his caste position and will not clean his work area. And the English foreman will be accommodating. Although these incidents are infrequent, word quickly gets around in the English community, causing puzzlement and resentment.

Other things also puzzle the host community. For example, many Punjabis dress shabbily and live in what the British consider sub-standard housing, giving the impression of being poverty-stricken when in fact some may have bank accounts of £10,000 or more. To the immigrants, good clothes and fancy houses are not a value, as they are for the white observer, whose attire denotes his class.

Punjabis have other misconceptions about life in England. They think injections are better medicine than tablets or syrups taken by mouth, and they believe that processed food is more nutritious than fresh food. As a result, one of the most common health problems among immigrant children is rickets. Doctors prescribe medicines and an egg a day for the child. Parents then provide but do not insure that the child eats, which baffles the doctor, who cannot understand why the child's condition is not improving.

Also, Punjabis do not understand that when medicine is prescribed, a full course should be administered. Generally, the Indian parents give the child the medication until there is a sign of improvement, then they stop the dosage without finishing the course. They usually blame the doctor if there is a relapse in the child's condition and still save the leftover medicine for future use for someone else.

The British tend to view all immigrants as one group, having the same problems and future. Thus, in talking with social workers and Community Relations officials, they assume that second generation Punjabis will fulfil the stereotype of young West Indians—an irresponsible, shiftless generation with a high crime, unemployment, and drug rate.[3] They fail to realize that the authority structure of the Punjabi family has remained intact and Punjabi behaviour is goal-oriented. Gravesindian children work hard to fulfil family goals. The host community is flooded with wrong information and misconceptions regarding the immigrant situation. Some or most of these fears can be alleviated through education; others can be dealt with by enlightened government policies and adequate use of mass media programmes.

The home village

Returning to Jandiali produces a shock—it is a ghost village. Including the inhabitants of Chamali, there are about 400 people left. The villagers claim that a family a week goes abroad.[4] Silence reigns in lane after lane where noises of children once echoed. Only locked doors greet the observer as he walks through the alleys.

Of those remaining in Jandiali, the bulk are primarily women, children, and old men. There are about five men between the ages of 19 and 50. This mass exodus is not all to England. Since 1972, labour opportunities have opened up in Dubai, Iran, and other Middle Eastern countries. While most of the Jats have gone to England, about 100 male Chamars and other specialist castes have grabbed the chance for enhancement and gone to these new areas of opportunity.

Like other villages in the Jullundur district, Jandiali has an 'external economy'; that is, it is supported by money sent by

emigrants. They have just completed a new gurdwara costing
Rs 1.3 lakhs, and have invested Rs 8 lakhs—primarily from
pounds donated by migrant villagers in England.[5] The Punjabis claim that money still comes back, but it is not to the same
extent as it used to be. For India in 1978 at least Rs 22,187 billion
(2,773 billion dollars), a 16 per cent increase over the previous
year, was sent back by overseas Indians—a large portion of this
came from the Middle East.

Most of Jandiali's emigrants own their land, which is cared
for by a friend or relative—many come to Jandiali from
Phagwara to oversee the fields of a relative in England. Holding
on to land is very important. About five new houses were built
recently which cost about a lakh of rupees each. Jandialians are
modernizing, with eight homes boasting flush toilets. In 1978
there was a television set and a telephone in the village—all of
which were unheard of in 1971.

The emigrants do not intend to relinquish their hold, and
play an active role in village affairs. After the old *Zaildar* of
Jandiali died, his family renovated the village gurdwara in
1977 in his memory without consulting other village leaders.
At about the same time, a group of emigrants donated money
to build a new village gurdwara to fulfil an emigrant's dream of
having a gurdwara tower so high that Phagwara could be seen
from its top. The village was divided. The *Zaildar*'s group re-
sisted the new construction. The emigrant faction, supported
strongly by non-Jat and poorer Jat families, pushed for the new
building. Finally, a compromise was reached which allowed
the new place of worship to be built. Now, morning prayers are
broadcast by each gurdwara in turn.

It was primarily the poorer element that had initially emigrated to England from Jandiali. Now their money gives them
power to decide village affairs. Most members of the emigrant
group are abroad and in 1978 their in-village representative
leader was about to join his son in Canada. This will leave the
faction without guidance.

The few inhabitants complain of Jandiali being a lonely
place and lacking in good labour—some of these labour needs
are supplied by migrants from Uttar Pradesh, but most Jat
farmers are resorting to mechanized farming. One Jat farmer
with his tractor cares for many acres of land, thus solving the
lack of labour problem.

In the case of immigrant villages like Jandiali, mostly Jats ventured abroad, usually to England, but now large segments of Chamars and other specialized castes such as Tarkhans and Lohars in particular are venturing to West Asia—sending money back and increasing the village wealth.

Urbanites in India are aware of racism abroad. They keenly watch the racial situation in Britain through newspapers, which give it good coverage. When Prime Minister James Callaghan visited India in January 1978, the press questioned him about the situation in Britain. Overseas Indians and their problems are a topic of research. Government officials differ as to how overseas Indians should be treated. There are some who feel that India should not be concerned about its expatriates and should not intervene on their behalf, whereas others claim that discrimination shows an inner contempt by the British toward their former colony so that the government should step in. Whatever the view, the fate of overseas Indians is a concern, whether they are of village or urban origin, educated or uneducated, of government official or private citizen.

There are double standards in this reporting. England is condemned for its racism, and yet nothing is said about turbaned Sikhs being barred from Saudi Arabia. The activities of the National Front are reported, while the counter-move of the Anti-Nazi League (an organization to combat the anti-immigrant policies of the National Front) has been completely ignored. In England, South Asian lecturers like Dr Bhikhu Parekh are quick to condemn discrimination in Britain, while completely ignoring the inequalities in their own country. And, when Indians, both in England and India, are confronted with this double standard, the reply often given resembled that of one Punjabi who said, 'But Britain is a civilized country. Inequality is not supposed to exist there as it does in our underdeveloped areas!' The standards they use for judging Great Britain are different from those used for judging themselves.

Many vital questions continue to go unanswered. What does the Punjabi in England desire? Does he want special programmes to account for the disadvantages he had to start with; that is, programmes of reverse discrimination? Does he feel that he should get preferential treatment because the English have robbed his homeland of its wealth? Does he think the host society should make it possible for him to mix more easily with British society? Or, does he want to be left alone? The expectations of the Punjabi community in Gravesend can be summed up in the words of one Sikh Jat who said, 'We only want two things from the British: assurance that we will not be kicked out, and freedom to work and move about without fear of harassment by racists. We ask for nothing more.'

APPENDIX A

SUMMARY OF STATISTICAL DATA ON JANDIALI

Total population (including members in Great Britain and
Chamali) 1,605

Total emigrants (Jandiali and Chamali) 515
    Africa 4
    Australia 1
    Canada 4
    Great Britain 402
    Malaya (military service) 2
    New Zealand 1
    Philippines 2
    United States of America 2
    Migrants within India 99

Chamali's population (including migrants) 309
    England emigrants 18
    Other emigrants 20

Jat population 830
    Jats in England 313
    Jat migrants within India 22
    Other emigrants 7

Land (total acreage) 646
    Acreage irrigated 555

Man–Land ratio 2.48 people per acre

Villages represented due to exogamous marriage rules 232
    (some as far away as Delhi and Calcutta)

APPENDIX B

COUNT OF INDIANS ABROAD[1]

Host Country	Number of Emigrants	Host Country	Number of Emigrants
Afghanistan	20,000	Greece	13
Aden	2,000	Guinea	5
Algeria	132	Guyana	342,374
Argentina	160	Hong Kong	4,000 to 5,000
Australia	3,108	Hungary	45
Austria	165	Indonesia	27,617
Bahrain	5,500	Iran	1,000
Barbados	512	Italy	761
Belgium	377	Iraq	12,570
Bolivia	5	Ireland	150
Botswana	400	Jamaica	27,951
Brazil	57	Japan	1,141
Bulgaria	nil	Jordan	39
Burma	272,000	Kenya	172,600
Burundi	175	Kuwait	12,006
Cambodia	80	Laos	1,800
Cameroun	20	Lebanon	250
Canada	20,000	Le Teunion	430
Sri Lanka	1,234,126	Libya	335
China	20	Liberia	325
Chile	63	Madagascar	12,350
Colombia	34	Malawi	10,900
Camores Island	85	Malaysia	810,000
Congo	3,000	Malta	100
Cuba	32	Mauritius	520,000
Cyprus	8	Mexico	20
Czechoslovakia	nil	Morocco	540
Dahomey	2	Muscat	4,500
Denmark	256	Netherlands	202
Ethiopia	4,520	New Zealand	6,130
Fiji	241,000	Nigeria	1,600
Finland	28	Norway	35
French Guiana	2	Panama	361
France	1,400	Philippines	2,516
Ghana	1,750	Poland	19
Gibraltar	150	Peru	10
Grenada	9,500	Qatar	2,000

[1] Since these 1970 figures were compiled, there has been a great deal of emigration from India, especially to the Middle East, Canada and the United States.

Host Country	Number of Emigrants	Host Country	Number of Emigrants
Rumania	1	Trinidad & Tobago	302,049
Rwanda	50	Togo	4
Saudi Arabia	1,035	Tonga	26
Senegal	73	Trucial States	5,000
Ivory Coast	1	Tunisia	27
Gambia	20	Turkey	11
Sierra-Leone	425	U.A.R.	453
Singapore	125,000	Uganda	76,000
Somalia	1,360	United Kingdom	321,995[1]
Southern Rhodesia	8,100	Uruguay	1
Spain	1,600	U.S.A.	32,062
St. Vincent	3,703	U.S.S.R.	759
Sudan	2,550	Venezuela	19
Surinam	101,715	Vietnam (North)	18
Switzerland	900	Vietnam (South)	2,000
Syria	10	West Germany	4,681
Tanzania	102,000	Yeman (North)	21
Thailand	18,014	Yugoslavia	95

Source: Shan 1970: 286–7.

[1] This is the 1971 census figure of Asians in Britain born within the boundaries of present-day India (those Indians born in what is now Pakistan or Bangladesh were excluded from this number). The 1978 estimate of individuals claiming South Asian origins in U.K., regardless of passport held, is 1.3 million. Thus there are about 900,000 individuals with ancestral beginnings in India (of which approximately 600,000 have a Punjabi heritage); and 400,000 claim Pakistan or Bangladesh as their ethnic home.

APPENDIX C

A 1971 CENSUS OF PIER ROAD: A PUNJABI STREET IN GRAVESEND

House No.	Adults M	Adults F	Children M	Children F	Comments	Home Village	Work	Relatives
21	1	1	1	3	1 family	Majha but born in Fiji	M—Greenhigh Paper F—Metropolitan Canister Company	*Male's*: 2 brothers & families, Gravesend; 1 brother & family, Derby *Female's*: 1 brother, Birmingham; 1 brother & family, Gravesend
23	3	3	2	2	3 nuclear families; 2 brothers having joint ownership; 3rd a lodger	Dhanowali	Construction, car parts factory, Maidstone; no wives working	*Male's*: 1 aunt in No. 76; 2 brothers-in-law in Wolverhampton & Swanscombe *Female's*: Brothers & sisters in Blackpool; brothers, No. 79; parents & relatives in Wolverhampton
24	3	3	1	3	1 extended family; 1 brother recently married, no children	Kher Achwal, Hoshiarpur	Old parents work for Urban Council, cleaning; sons work Amalgamated Elec. Ind. Paper Sack Factory, Northfleet;	Parents in Southall

A 1971 CENSUS OF PIER ROAD—*continued*

House No.	Adults M	Adults F	Children M	Children F	Comments	Home Village	Work	Relatives
26	5	2	1	2	2 families in joint ownership	Cheema Rapur	Construction	
27	3	3	3	3	3 brothers with families. House owned by No. 48. Wife's brother, sister-in-law with her child lodges here also		Imperial Paper Mill, across river	*Female's:* brother in Northfleet
41					Owned by No. 48 and rented to 4 families; composition unknown			
44	3	3	2	2	Joint ownership between 2 friends	Chibewal	Construction near Nakador	
48	4	3	2	1	Joint ownership between man and nephew, but 3 nuclear families	Dhanowali Manko Moranwali	Empire Paper Mill Lumber Mill, Maidstone	*Male's:* wife and son in Sunderland w/English daughter-in-law. Daughter studying; parents in Gravesend. Father came in 1939. Cousin in No. 79 *Female's:* 2 brothers, Gravesend; brother & 4 sons, Gravesend

A 1971 CENSUS OF PIER ROAD—*continued*

House No.	Adults M	F	Children M	F	Comments	Home Village	Work	Relatives
51	4	3	2		Owner rents to 2 families and 1 single lodger	Dhanowali, Ludhiana	Empire Paper Mill; Wife—Dartford Laundry	*Male's*: Second wife in India. *Female's*: Sister in No. 76. Uncle & aunt, Gravesend
59	1		2			Aulak	Construction	*Male's*: Wife in India with children visiting. Cousin in No. 91. Cousin, Gravesend. Brother, Gravesend. Uncle in No. 79. Wife's cousin, Gravesend
69	1	1	2					
70	1	1	2	1		Bir Pind	Construction College, Dartford Laundry	
72	2	2	2	2	Family of 6 with nephew	Pharala	Bata; Amalgamate Elec. Co.; Greenwithe Brick Factory; Grays	*Male's*: Village-mate, Gravesend
74	1	1	2	1	Levirate marriage, 1st wife dead	Nava Pind, Jullundur	Zinc Oxide, Dartford. Wife not working	*Male's*: 1 son in India. Sister's sons, No. 23. Sister's sister-in-law, No. 76. Cousin, Glasgow. Father, Panama

A 1971 CENSUS OF PIER ROAD—*continued*

House No.	Adults M	Adults F	Children M	Children F	Comments	Home Village	Work	Relatives
75	4	2	5	1	4-generation family, came in World War II	Chechen, Jullundur	Dockyards, Chathbay; Zinc Oxide, Dartford; Empire Paper Mill; Post Office, London; Electric lineman	*Male's:* Niece, No. 76. Daughter & family, Bradford. Brother, Gravesend.
76	1	1	1	1	Daughter in college.	Dhenowali Serai Khas near Kartarpur	Bowater; Bata. Car parts factory. College	*Male's:* Brother, No. 77. *Female's:* Sister, Birmingham. Widowed sister-in-law, Taplow, Buckinghamshire. Uncle in Gravesend. Cousin, No. 48. Sister & brother-in-law, No. 74. Nephew, No. 23. Brother, No. 51. Uncle, No. 75.
77	3	2		2	Hindu couple—lodgers	Sarai Khas, Kartarpur	Northfleet Power Station	*Male's:* Brother, No. 76. *Female's:* Cousin, Birmingham. Cousin, No. 78
78	1	2		2			Bowater Paper Mills. Wife not working	*Male's:* Cousin, No. 77. Sister in Leeds, York. *Female's:* Aunts, uncles, cousins in Southall

A 1971 CENSUS OF PIER ROAD—*continued*

House No.	Adults M	Adults F	Children M	Children F	Comments	Home Village	Work	Relatives
79	2	2	4	1	2 brothers with family	Mozara, Jullundur	Construction	*Male's*: Sister, No. 23. *Female's*: Relatives, Birmingham
80	1	1	2	1	Hindu	Shankar, Jullundur	Amalgamate Elec. Construction. Student at Tech. College	*Male's*: Brother & father, Gravesend
85	2	1	2	3		Kariewal	Empire Paper Mill	*Male's*: Aunt, Birmingham
86	2	2		1	Parents and married son w/younger son	Raikot		
91	1	1	3	3		Oujala	Greenhigh Paper Mills. Bata Shoe Company.	*Male's*: Nephew, Gravesend. Nephew, Barking Essex. Cousin, No. 55. Cousin, Gravesend.
93	4	1			Family and 2 men tenants	Batala	Bata. Brick factory; Grays	*Male's*: 2 sons studying in India.

GLOSSARY

Adharmi sweepers

Akhand Kirtan Jatha a Sikh sect that emphasizes purity, singing, and meditation

Akhand Path perfect or complete worship; as used here, it is a continuous reading of the *Guru Granth Sahib* (the holy book of the Sikhs)

Angraiz a respectable term for an Englishman

Atta whole wheat flour

Bara Sahib important person

Baisakhi spring harvest festival for Punjabis

Bhatras a pedlar group in Punjab

Bazigar performer, acrobat

Bébé grandmother, father's mother

Bhabi brother's wife

Bhangi sweeper

Biradari brotherhood, fraternity, connection, kindred

Brahmins priests

Chacha father's brother

Chamar caste of leather-workers

Chamali low-caste housing area

Chowkidar watchman

Chota little

Doaba the land between two rivers; as used in this study, it refers to the Jullundur Doab

Five K's the five symbols worn by the Sikhs; they include *Kes* (hair), *Karha* (steel bracelet), *Kirpan* (sword), *Kangha* (comb), and *Kachha* (shorts)

Gora a term sometimes used derogatorily for the white man

Granth Sahib see *Guru Granth Sahib*

Ghar-javai literally, a house son-in-law. This is a derogatory term used for a man who resides with his wife's parents.

Granthi priest or reader of a holy book

Gurbani holy words

Gurmukhi   script of the Sikhs

Guru Granth Sahib or *Granth Sahib*   the holy book of the Sikhs

Izzat   honour, respectability, esteem, grandeur

Izzatwali   from a family with izzat

Jaidad   wealth

Jawan   soldier

Jheer   water carriers

Kabaddi   a competitive Indian sport

Kachha   shorts, a Sikh symbol

Kameez   loose top shirt

Kangha   comb, a Sikh symbol

Karha   steel bracelet, a Sikh symbol

Kaur   princess, the last name given to all Sikh women.

Kes   hair, a Sikh symbol

Khalsa   the soldier-saint brotherhood of believers adhering to Sikhism

Khidmat   hospitality, service

Kirpan   sword, a Sikh symbol

Kumhar   potter

Lohar   ironsmith

Mann   the more familiar term used by Doaba villagers concerning izzat; see izzat

Marasi   musician

Muhabbat   love and affection, devotion

Pirhi   generation

Pukka   strong or firm

Ramgardiahs   carpenters

Robh   power

Sardar   a leader. A respectful term used to address a Sikh

Sarpanch   headman of the panchayat

Sat Sri Akal   Sikh greeting (in the name of truth)

Seva   service

Singh   lion, the name given to most Sikh men

Sadharan Path   simple reading (a non-continuous reading of the *Guru Granth Sahib*)

Sunyar   goldsmith

Zaildar   superintendent of several villages

These spellings and definitions may vary from one region to another.

NOTES

CHAPTER I THE PEOPLE STUDIED: PUNJABIS, SIKHS AND JATS

1 Although there are no official statistics, Hiro (1971:9) and Rose (1969:52), travel agents in India and South Asian immigrants in Britain, agree with the above estimate. Jullundur is the largest supplier of migrants to Britain, followed by Hoshiarpur and Kapurthala (see Figure 2). Ludhiana ranks fourth because many of those from this region went to Africa.

2 Claiming Kshatriya membership, however, is a common tactic used by groups in India to enhance their social ranking (Srinivas 1968:190).

3 Although Sikhs have made a strong contribution to the Indian military before and after independence, these villagers perceive governmental bureaucrats as exploitive—a group not to trust but to manipulate.

4 West Punjab refers to the sector of Punjab in Pakistan, and East Punjab refers to the unit in India.

5 Doaba in this study will refer only to the Jullundur Doab.

CHAPTER II THE CULTURAL CONTEXT

1 In the case of the Sikh Jats, assassination is a threat to induce deviant girls to conform to communal norms.

2 The Punjabi term *mann* is commonly used by rural Punjabis when referring to the concept of honour. However, since the term 'izzat' is commonly resorted to in South Asian literature, this study will use izzat rather than *mann*.

3 The Indian government in the 1960s and early 1970s only allowed a person to exchange the equivalent of £3.

4 Part of this is due to the gross misperception Indians have of western culture. For example, in village India, my wife and I were often quizzed about our marital relationship—the villagers' perception was that westerners rarely marry, but freely have sex with anyone they fancy.

5 This study uses the term 'case' as a means of presentation that deduces information from the narrative.

6 All identities are disguised.

7 To the villagers, a humble person serves others and is publicly recognized for this service. According to Punjabi concepts, humility does not require operating in secret.

CHAPTER III EMIGRATION STARTS

1 'Phoren' means foreign in idiomatic Punjabi.
2 Of the numerous contacts contributing to the study, no Jat has been known to sell or mortgage his land to go to England or send a son to England.
3 Leaving one's wife is a traditional Punjabi tactic for an unhappily married man.

CHAPTER IV THE BIRTH OF GRAVESINDIA (1947–1959)

1 A term of use here to refer to the Indian community within Gravesend.
2 This is in contrast to the Bedford Indian community, where about one-half of the 1,000 Indians are untouchables (Brown 1970:117). Most of the Gravesindian Sikh Jat population is from Doaba; although not from the same village, they knew about one another through the open channels of inter-village communication in Punjab. The villages that provided most of the Gravesend Indian community are Paragpur, Jandiali, Jandiala, Moranwali, Palahi, Shankar, Serai, Dhanowali, Rurka, and Thankarki, which are primarily located near and around the cities of Phagwara, Jullundur, Hoshiarpur, and Ludhiana.
3 Due to a shortage of teachers in England during the 1960s, Punjabi school teachers (both men and women) were hired despite their Punjab University degree and training. Some Punjabis teach in all white schools.
4 Indians generally do not patronize restaurants; hence, this restaurant caters to an English clientele.
5 Bowater Scott Paper Company.
6 No one was ever sure exactly when this desired wealth was accumulated.
7 Rs 36 to £1 was the approximate black market rate at that time. Rs 18 to £1 was the official rate of exchange.
8 In these early years men did not write home negative reports about each other.
9 I found this hard to believe until I actually saw a man's pay cheque, which showed that he had logged 90 hours of work that week. The Punjabis claim that this is common, and from what was observed, it is believable. They were, and still are, obsessed with making more money.
10 A Sikh celebration of the continuous reading of the Granth Sahib to mark a holy day, happy or sad occasion.
11 Emigration during these early years brought few people from Jandiali and Punjab. Before 1950, about 10 men had emigrated; the Punjabi population in Gravesend in the mid-1950s was between 350 and 400. With the initial threat and later passage of the 1962 Immigration Act, the immigrant population rapidly increased to 2,000 by 1962 and then steadily increased to the present (1971) figure of about 5,600.
12 In the 1960s and early 1970s, it was common to refer to non-whites, even by Gravesindians, as Pakistanis. Hence, the terms 'Paki bashing' and 'Paki girls'.

CHAPTER V BEATING THE BAN ON IMMIGRATION
(1960–1962)

1 For further details, see Appendix C.

2 Joint residence is common in India. In fact, it is usually an economic necessity. To the Jat in England, one nuclear family to a house was a waste of space. Privacy and individual rooms were not a value held by most Indians. In fact, they had probably never experienced it. What the westerner termed over-crowding was normal living for the Jat from rural Punjab.

3 Being a store operator no longer seemed to have the stigma that it had in the early years. The reason behind this change in evaluation is clarified when the change in the significance of Jat wealth which occurred in the later years of the migrants' stay in England is discussed.

4 There is a frightening truth in the fact that this comment applies, after more than a hundred years, to the same setting that inspired Dickens to write about working conditions in English industry.

CHAPTER VI STAYING LONGER (1963–1971)

1 Kim Bhojwani was in Gravesend for a very short time. Kim gained Jat respect and a following because of his educational background and fluent English.

2 Council housing consists of apartment complexes run by the government for low-income families.

3 The Commonwealth Immigrants Act of 1962 required all prospective immigrants to obtain labour vouchers from the British Ministry of Labour. There were three categories of vouchers: 'A' for those with a specific job, 'B' for those with special qualifications, and 'C' for all others. The 'C' category was eventually discontinued, but while the system was in effect, the proportion of educated Punjabis immigrating into England increased.

4 The non-western analogy for old peoples' homes.

5 Although this conviction was later reversed on a technicality, this narrator illustrates the power an interpreter had at that time.

6 The Community Relations Council (CRC) was a governmental organization to promote harmony between ethnic groups in Gravesend. Encouraged by the nationally created Community Relations Commission, the name was changed in 1977 to the Commission for Racial Equality. Such groups were formed in communities throughout Britain where minority populations were present.

7 These political groups resemble factions in that they centre on one individual as a leader, such as described by Nicholas (1965:21–62), and yet the leader's position depends on his having a strong kin group in the community to back him; a structure resembling Mayer's (1966:97–122) description of the quasi-kin group.

8 The terms 'kingmaker' and 'broker' are analytical categories used to explain what was observed. The other categories were used by the Punjabis themselves.

9 See John (1969) and Desai (1963).

10 The Indian Workers' Association, founded in Coventry in 1938 (John 1969:

43), did not have a major impact in Gravesend until 1966 when a chapter was founded.

11   Forcibly cutting a victim's beard or stealing his turban was a common means of humiliating an opponent.

12   This has since undergone change because the present law allows spouses of both sexes to be sponsored. Therefore, the English-Punjabi girl is also in great demand by potential immigrants.

13   This situation is changing. The birth rate in the Punjabi community is rapidly declining.

14   Gravesindians who experienced discriminatory treatment are very emphatic in their contempt for the English.

15   At the time of this study, Rs 7.50 were equivalent to the dollar and about Rs 15 were equivalent to a pound.

16   A village further south received emigrant money deposits in their cooperative bank of over Rs 2 million in two years.

17   A good example is Nihal Singh's article in the Delhi *Statesman* (1971:14) that tells of the possibility of unjust deportation of Indians from Britain; Lawson's article on 'British Immigrants' (*The Statesman* 1971) explains that the Asians were on the firing line instead of the Caribbeans as had previously been the case. There are other eye-catching titles in Indian newspapers: 'Keeping Britain White' (*The Statesman*, 22 October 1971); '15 Start Dharna for Entry Permits to UK' (*The Tribune*, 14 October 1971); 'Labour Club Bars Coloured' (*The Statesman*, 27 March 1975); and so on.

CHAPTER VII   FACING THE FUTURE

1   Of these forty-two, there were seven old men, two ladies (one of them my wife), three children, and six representatives of the Indian Youth Federation; the rest were middle-aged men from all walks of life who were concerned with the higher education of their children. The absence of women does not indicate a lack of concern or influence on their part. As always for Punjabis, the power of the women is hidden; the desires of the wives of the men present were undoubtedly followed during the debate.

2   What follows is an edited transcript of speeches and behaviour.

3   GCE stands for General Certificate of Education. 'O' levels are ordinary level examinations which are taken by children between the ages of 15 and 18 years.

4   'A' levels are advanced level examinations taken by children in the sixth form. Passing 'A' level exams facilitates matriculation to University in England.

5   A Hindi term meaning white. *Gora* is usually a derogatory term used by the Punjabi to refer to the whites. It is comparable to the term 'nigger' or 'whitie'. Punjabis use the word *Angraiz* to refer to the English in a more respectful manner.

6   Apart from the language, one of the main differences between the English and Punjabi educational systems is that in Punjab, emphasis is usually on rote learning rather than attempts at original reasoning as in the British system. A Punjabi student reads the text, memorizes the main points, and regurgitates them for exams.

7   He included those going to technical school in this number.

8   About nine parents in Gravesend who could afford it sent their children to the Khalsa public schools in Dehra Dun and Nabha to get a good foundation without exposure to the bad influence of *goras*.

9   This meeting was held while the 1971 Immigration bill was being debated in Parliament.

10 One of the biggest complaints of the Punjabi community is that children are given neither homework nor the opportunity to study at home because their books are kept in school.

11 Term used to quiet a bedlam, literally 'Say loudly in the name of God.'

12 *Sat Sri Akal* is a response which means 'God is truth'. It is also the Sikh greeting used to say 'hello' and 'good-bye'.

13 Elsewhere in England, especially among Punjabi women in the larger cities, trousers were popular. Culturally they are acceptable, for they cover the legs.

CHAPTER VIII   WHY STAY IN ENGLAND?

1   Lawyers with LLB degrees from Punjab University and some who were Barristers-at-law in a city.

2   Balwant Singh, a dissatisfied immigrant, has since attempted twice more to live in India, but each time has lost his assets in poor investments, and returned.

3   To these Punjabi Sikh Jat emigrants from Jandiali, India is Punjab. For example, one English school teacher asked a non-Punjabi South Asian lady to talk to the class about India. The Punjabi girls in the class emphatically insisted that the guest was not from India for she was not wearing a salwar-kameez, she was wearing a sari, a dress with which they were not acquainted. A Punjabi Jat at a Gravesindian community celebration announced that he was going to sing a song about Mother India, but proceeded to sing about Mother Punjab.

4   While emotional blackmail might well be a universal tactic, it is employed openly in Punjabi culture. Frequently, many members of the community are called upon to aid in this practice.

EPILOGUE (1972–1978)

1   There is a National Front Party in Gravesend.

2   This estimate is based on figures given by Gravesindians.

3   I am not qualified to discuss West Indian behaviour. What is related here is a stereotype communicated to me in interviews.

4   This is unlikely, however, for if such were the case, the village would have been empty long ago.

5   The proceeds from this company are used to finance emigration.

SELECT BIBLIOGRAPHY

PUNJABI AND INDIAN CULTURE

AHLUWALIA, M. M.
1965   *Kukas: The Freedom Fighters of Punjab.* New Delhi: Allied Publishers Private Limited.

AHMAD, SAGHIR
1967   'Class and Power in the Punjabi Village'. East Lansing: Michigan State University, Ph.D. Dissertation.

1974   'A Village in Pakistani Punjab: Jalpana', in Clarence Maloney (ed.), *South Asia: Seven Community Profiles.* New York: Holt, Rinehart, & Winston.

BAILEY, F. G.
1963   'Closed Social Stratification in India', in *Archives de Europes Sociology*, IV, pp. 107–24.

BAJWA, FAUJA SINGH
1965   *Kuka Movement.* Delhi: Motilal Banarsidas.

BARTH, FREDRIK
1959   *Political Leadership Among Swat Pathans.* New York: Humanities Press, Inc.

1960   'The System of Social Stratification in Swat, North Pakistan', in E. R. Leach (ed.), *Aspects of Caste in South India, Ceylon, and North-West Pakistan.* Cambridge: Cambridge University Press.

BEDI, SOHINDER SINGH
1971   *Folklore of Punjab.* New Delhi: National Book Trust, India.

CHHABRA, G. S.
1968   *Advanced History of the Punjab*, Vols. I & II. Jullundur: New Academic Publishing Co.

COLE, W. OWEN and PIARA SINGH SAMBHI
1978   *The Sikhs: Their Religious Beliefs and Practices.* London: Routledge & Kegan Paul.

COLLINS, LARRY and DOMINIQUE LA PIERRE
1975   *Freedom at Midnight.* New York: Simon and Schuster.

CROOK, W.
n.d.   *Races of Northern India.* Delhi: Cosmo Publications.

DARLING, MALCOLM LYALL
1925   *The Punjab Peasant in Prosperity and Debt.* Bombay: Oxford University Press.

1966   *Apprentice to Power: India 1904–1908.* London: The Hogarth Press.

DUMONT, L.
1966   *Homo Heirarchicus: The Caste System and its Implications.* London: Weidenfeld and Nicolson.

DUMONT, L. and D. POCOCK

1958   *Contributions to Indian Sociology*, Vol. II, April. The Hague, Mouton & Co.

EDWARDES, ALLEN

1959   *The Jewel and the Lotus*. New York: Lance Books.

EGLER, ZEKIYE

1957   'Punjabi Village Life', in *Pakistan: Society and Culture*. New Haven: Human Relations Area Files.

1960   *A Punjabi Village in Pakistan*. New York: Columbia University Press.

GERTH, H. H. and C. WRIGHT MILLS

1946   *From Max Weber: Essays in Sociology*. New York: Oxford University Press.

GUPTA, SHER SINGH

1977   *Agriculture in Punjab*. Chandigarh: Public Relations Department.

HARPER, EDWARD

1964   'Ritual Pollution and an Integrator of Caste and Religion', in Edward Harper (ed.), *Religion in South Asia*. Seattle: University of Washington Press.

HELWEG, ARTHUR W.

1970   'Punjabi Peasant Society, A Study in Summary Structure'. East Lansing: Michigan State University, M.A. Thesis.

HONIGMANN, JOHN J.

1958   *Three Pakistan Villages*. Chapel Hill: Institute for Research in Social Sciences, University of North Carolina.

HUTTON, J. G.

1963   *Caste in India*. 4th edition. Oxford: Oxford University Press.

KESSINGER, TOM G.

1974   *Vilyatpur 1848–1968: Social and Economic Change in a North Indian Village*. Berkeley: University of California Press.

LATIF, SYED MUHAMMAD

1964   *History of the Punjab*. New Delhi: Eurasia Publishing House (Pvt.) Ltd.

LEAF, MURRAY J.

1972   *Information and Behavior in a Sikh Village: Social Organization Reconsidered*. Berkeley: University of California Press.

LEWIS, OSCAR

1958   *Village Life in Northern India: Studies in a Delhi Village*. Urbana: University of Illinois Press.

LYNCH, OWEN M.

1968   'The Politics of Untouchability—A Case from Agra, India', in Milton Singer and Bernard Cohn (eds.), *Structure and Change in Indian Society*. Chicago: Aldine Publishing Company.

1969   *The Politics of Untouchability*. New York: Columbia University Press.

MADDICK, HENRY

1970   *Panchayati Raj: A Study of Rural Local Government in India*. London: Longman.

MAJUMDAR, B. N.

1965   *Military System of the Sikhs*. New Delhi: S. Attar Singh, Prop. Army Educational Stores.

MALONEY, CLARENCE
 1974 *Peoples of South Asia*. New York: Holt, Rinehart, & Winston.
MANDELBAUM, DAVID
 1972 *Society in India: Continuity and Change*. Berkeley: University of California Press.
MARRIOTT, McKIM
 1955 *Village India*. Chicago: The University of Chicago Press.
 1968 'Caste Ranking and Food Transactions: A Matrix Analysis', in Milton Singer and Bernard Cohn (eds.), *Structure and Change in Indian Society*. Chicago: Aldine Publishing Co., pp. 133–71.
MASON, PHILIP
 1974 *A Matter of Honour: An Account of the Indian Army, Its Officers and Men*. Harmondsworth: Penguin Books.
MEHTA, VED
 1957 *Face to Face*. New York: Little Brown and Company.
 1972 *Daddyji*. New York: Farrar, Straus & Giroux.
OPLER, MORRIS and RUDRA DATT SINGH
 1964 'The Division of Labor in an Indian Village', in Carelton S. Coon (ed.), *A Reader in General Anthropology*. New York: Holt, Rinehart, & Winston, pp. 464–96.
PETTIGREW, JOYCE
 1972 'Some Observations on the Social System of Sikh Jats', in *New Community*. Vol. 1, No. 5.
 1975 *Robber Noblemen: A Study of the Political System of the Sikh Jats*. London: Routledge & Kegan Paul.
PUNJAB
 1908 *Imperial Gazetteer of India*. Provincial Series, Punjab. Vols. 1 & 2. Calcutta: Superintendent of Government Printing.
 1970 *Statistical Abstract of Punjab*. Government of Punjab (India). Issued by the Economic Adviser to the Government. Punjab: Chandigarh.
 1977 *Punjab Shows the Way*. Chandigarh: Public Relations Department, Government of Punjab.
ROSE, H. A.
 1919 *A Glossary of the Tribes and Castes of the Punjab and Northwest Frontier Province*. Vols. 1, 2, & 3. Patiala: Languages Department of Punjab.
SABERWAL, SATISH
 1972 'Status, Mobility, and Networks in a Punjabi Industrial Town', in Satish Saberwal (ed.), *Beyond the Village*. Simla: Indian Institute of Advanced Study, pp. 111–84.
SARHADI, AJIT SINGH
 1970 *Punjabi Suba: The Story of the Struggle*. Delhi: U. C. Kapur & Sons.
SHAN, LAL (ED.)
 1970 *The Times of India Directory and Yearbook* (including Who's Who 1970). Bombay: The Times of India Press.
SHINDE, A. K.
 1971 'Punjab Alone Will Wipe Out Rice Deficit in Two Years.' Chandigarh: *The Tribune*, Saturday, 4 September 1971, p. 12.

Singh, Avtar
   1970   *Ethics of the Sikhs*. Patiala: Punjabi University.

Singh, Fuja
   1969   *The Military System of the Sikhs*.

Singh, Khazan
   1914a   *History of the Sikh Religion*. Chandigarh: Department of Languages, Government of Punjab.
   1914b   *Philosophy of the Sikh Religion*. Chandigarh: Department of Languages, Government of Punjab.

Singh, Khushwant
   1956   *Train to Pakistan*. London: Greenwood.
   1959   *The Sikhs Today*. Bombay: Orient Longmans.
   1963   *A History of the Sikhs*. Vol. 1. Princeton: Princeton University Press.
   1966   *A History of the Sikhs*. Vol. 2. Princeton: Princeton University Press.

Smith, Marian W.
   1952   'The Misal: A Structural Village-Group of India and Pakistan', in *American Anthropologist*, 54:41–56.

Spate, O. H. K. and A. T. A. Learmonth
   1967   *India and Pakistan*. London: Methuen & Co., Ltd.

Srinivas, M. N.
   1968   'Mobility in the Caste System', in Milton Singer and Bernard Cohn (eds.), *Structure and Change in Indian Society*. Chicago: Aldine Publishing Company, pp. 189–200.

Suri, C. S.
   1970   *Punjab District Gazetteers*. Ludhiana, Chandigarh: Government of Punjab.
   1971   *Punjab Through the Ages*. Chandigarh: Punjabi Ithihas Prakashan.

Talyarkhan, A. F. S.
   1971   'Sikhs in Sports', in *The Illustrated Weekly of India*. Bombay. Vol. XCII, Sunday, 31 October, pp. 44–5.

Tandon, Prakash
   1961   *Punjabi Century*. New York: Harcourt, Brace & World.

Temple, R. C.
   1884   *The Legends of the Punjab*. Vols. I, II & III. Patiala: Language Department, Punjab.

Wyon, J. B. and J. E. Gordon
   1971   *The Khanna Study: Population Problems in the Rural Punjab*. Cambridge (Mass.): Harvard University Press.

SOUTH ASIANS ABROAD

Arasartnan, Sinnapah
   1970   *Indians in Malaysia and Singapore*. London: Oxford University Press for the Institute of Race Relations.

Aurora, G. S.
   1967   *The New Frontiersmen*. Bombay: Popular Prakashan.

BALLARD, CATHERINE
 1978   'Arranged Marriages in the British Context', in *New Community*. Vol. 6, No. 3.

BALLARD, R.
 1972-3 'Family Organization among the Sikhs in Britain', in *New Community*. Vol. 2, No. 1.

BEETHAM, DAVID
 1970   *Transport and Turbans: A Comparative Study in Local Politics*. London: Oxford University Press for the Institute of Race Relations.

BENEDICT, BURTON
 1965   *Mauritius: Problems of the Plural Society*. London: Pall Mall Press for the Institute of Race Relations.

BHARATI, A.
 1972   *Asians in East Africa*. Chicago: Nelson Hall.

BRATA, SASTHI
 1978   Sasthi Brata's 'London Notebook', in *The Statesman*. Calcutta: 7 January 1978, p. 8.

BROOKS, DENNIS and KARAMJIT SINGH
 1978-9 'Ethnic Commitment Versus Structural Reality: South Asian Immigrant Workers in Britain', in *New Community*. Vol. 7, No. 1.

DAHYA, BADR
 1972-3 'Pakistanis in England', in *New Community*. Vol. 2, No. 1.
 1973   'Pakistanis in Britain: Transients or Settlers?' In *Race*. Vol. 14, No. 3.
 1974   'The Nature of Pakistani Ethnicity in Industrial Cities in Britain', in Abner Cohen (ed.), *A.S.A. Monograph No. 12*, Urban Ethnicity. London: Tavistock.

DESAI, RASHMI
 1963   *Indian Immigrants in Britain*. London: Oxford University Press for the Institute of Race Relations.

DINES, MARY; BIPLAB DASGUPTA; FRANK LEE; BRIAN DONNELLY; and JASWANT SINGH ATWAL
 1977   'Racism in the United Kingdom: The Myths, the Truths and the Task Ahead', in *The Hindu*. Madras: 28 December 1977, pp. 7-9.

HIRO, DILIP
 1967   *The Indian Family in Britain*. London: Community Relations Commission. Revised 1972.
 1971   'Going to Phoren', in *The Illustrated Weekly of India*. Bombay: Vol. 92, No. 44 (31 October 1971), pp. 8-13.

JEFFERY, PATRICIA
 1976   *Migrants and Refugees: Muslim and Christian Families in Bristol*. Cambridge: Cambridge University Press.

JOHN, DEWITT, JR.
 1969   *Indian Workers' Association in Britain*. London: Oxford University Press for the Institute of Race Relations.

KONDAPI, C.
 1951   *Indians Overseas: 1838-1949*. New Delhi, Indian Council of World Affairs. London: Oxford University Press.

KUSHNER, GILBERT
    1973   *Immigrants from India in Israel.* Tucson: The University of Arizona Press.

LAWSON, NIGEL
    1971   'Britain's Immigrants: Different Roads to Power', in *The Statesman.* New Delhi: 22 December 1971.

MARSH, PETER
    1967   *The Anatomy of a Strike.* Institute of Race Relations. Special Series.

NOWIKOWSKI, SUSAN and ROBIN WARD
    1978–9   'Middle Class and British?—An Analysis of South Asians in Suburbia', in *New Community.* Vol. 7, No. 1.

SHARMA, URSULA
    1971   *Rampal and His Family.* London: Collins.

SINGH, AMAR KUMAR
    1963   *Indian Students in Britain: A Survey of their Amusements and Attitudes.* New York: Asia Publishing House.

SINGH, KIRPAL
    1971   *The Sikh Symbols.* Gravesend: The Sikh Missionary Society U.K.

SINGH, NIHAL
    1971   'Race Relations Worsen in Britain', in *The Statesman.* New Delhi: 23 July 1971, p. 14.

THOMPSON, M.
    1974   'The Second Generation—Punjabi or English?', in *New Community.* Vol. 3, No. 3.

TINKER, HUGH
    1974   *A New System of Slavery: The Export of Indian Labour Overseas 1830–1920.* London: Oxford University Press for the Institute of Race Relations.
    1976   *Separate and Unequal.* London: C. Hurst.
    1977   *The Banyan Tree: Overseas Emigrants from India, Pakistan and Bangladesh.* Oxford: Oxford University Press.

UNSIGNED
    1971   'Keeping Britain White', in *The Statesman.* New Delhi: 22 October 1971.
    1971   '15 Start Dharna for Entry Permits to UK', in *The Tribune.* Chandigarh: 14 October 1971.
    1974   'Back to Work at Imperial', in *Race Today.* September, pp. 249–51.
    1975   'Labour Club Bars Coloured', in *The Statesman.* New Delhi: 27 March 1975.
    1978   'Mrs Thatcher's Bold Gamble', in *Time* (Europe). 20 February 1978, pp. 14–15.
    1978   'Angry Reaction in Britain over Racist; Acquittal', in *The Sunday Statesman.* New Delhi: 8 January 1978, p. 7.
    1978   'Mc Kinnon's Law'. In *The Economist.* Vol. 266, No. 7011, p. 15.

BRITISH RACIAL SITUATION

ANWAR, MUHAMMAD
  1976   *Between Two Cultures*: A Study of Relationships *Between Generations in the Asian Community in Britain.* London: Community Relations Commision.

BROWN, JOHN
  1970   *The Un-Melting Pot: An English Town and Its Immigrants.* London: Macmillan.

DAVIDSON, R. B.
  1966   *Black British: Immigrants to England.* London: Oxford University Press for the Institute of Race Relations.

DEAKIN, NICHOLAS
  1970   *Colour, Citizenship and British Society.* London: Panther Books.

HIRO, DILIP
  1971   *Black British, White British.* New York and London: Monthly Review Press, Revised 1973.

REX, JOHN and ROBERT MOORE
  1969   *Race, Community and Conflict: A Study of Sparkbrook.* London: Oxford University Press for the Institute of Race Relations.

ROSE, E. J. B.
  1969   *Colour and Citizenship: A Report on British Race Relations.* London: Oxford University Press.

SMITH, DAVID
  1977   *Racial Disadvantage in Britain: The PEP Report.* Harmondsworth: Penguin Books.

STEEL, DAVID
  1969   *No Entry: The Background and Implications of the Commonwealth Immigrants Act, 1968.* London: C. Hurst.

TWITCHIN, JOHN (ED.)
  1978   *Five Views of Multi-Racial Britain.* London: Commission for Racial Equality.

MISCELLANEOUS

BENEDICT, BURTON
  1968   'Family Firms and Economic Development', in *Southwestern Journal of Anthropology.* Vol. 24, No. 1.

GRAVESEND
  1969–   *Gravesend Official Handbook 1969–70.* London: Edward J. Borrow &
  1970   Co., Ltd., Publishers.

HISOCK, ROBERT H.
  1976   *A History of Gravesend.* London and Chichester: Phillmore & Co., Ltd.

MAYER, ADRIAN
  1966   'The Significance of Quasi-Groups in the Study of Complex Societies', in Michael Banton (ed.), *Association for Social Anthropologists Monograph No. 6.* London: Tavistock Publications.

MERTON, ROBERT K.
    1968   *Social Theory and Social Structure*. New York: The Free Press.
NICHOLAS, RALPH W.
    1965   'Factions: a Comparative Analysis', in Michael Banton (ed.), *Association for Social Anthropologists Monograph No. 2*. London: Tavistock Publications.
PERISTIANY, J. G. (ED.)
    1966   *Honour and Shame: The Values of Mediterranean Society*. Chicago: The University of Chicago Press.
SAHLINS, MARSHALL D.
    1965   'On the Sociology of Primitive Exchange', in Michael Banton (ed.), *The Relevance of Models for Social Anthropology. The Association for Social Anthropologists Monograph No. 2*. London: Tavistock Publications.
WATSON, JAMES L.
    1977   *Between Two Cultures: Migrants and Minorities in Britain*. Oxford: Basil Blackwell.
YOUNG, MICHAEL and PETER WILMOTT
    1957   *Family and Kinship in East London*. Baltimore, Md.: Penguin Books.

INDEX